Mind Training For Swimmers

-*Everything You Need To Know*-

Written by Craig Townsend

Bellissima Publishing, LLC
Jamul, California

This book is one person's opinion only and is not intended to give specific psychological or medical advice of any kind, for specific advise, please see your own psychologist, physiatrist , health advisor or doctor.

Copyright © 2005 by Craig Twonsend

IBSN 0-9771916-8-0

First Edition

Mind Training For Swimmers

-Everything You Need To Know-

Table of Contents

I dedicate this book to my wife Michelle,
who extracts the positives from every life situation
and sees the highest good in all people.

I would also like to sincerely thank:
Penny Weigand from California
for her endless assistance with the publishing of this book.

Denise Hecht from Atlanta, Georgia
for her wisdom, friendship and support.

Stuart Meares from Sydney, Australia
for his kind assistance, interest and patience.

CHAPTER 1

Mental Training - The Ultimate Secret Weapon

Welcome to "Mind Training for Swimmers - Everything You Need To Know." You have come to the right place. This book is designed to give you all the knowledge and techniques required to improve your swimming times and performance, and give you that extra boost of power you've been seeking. And that is exactly what I intend to do, with your help.

This book will provide many things - a mental training program, knowledge of all kinds of powerful techniques, the mind/body connection explained, ways to overcome short and long-term problems and *mentally protecting* yourself from swimmers who would like to bring you down.

This book delves deeply into the mind of the swimmer, but more importantly, provides a simple but very powerful program for you to follow. I will show you exactly *how* to use each technique to its fullest

Mind Training for Swimmers

capability - and also provide the recommended *repetitions and time periods* required for each technique.

There is far too much information in this book for you to use all at once - all you need to do is follow the exact mental training program I set you, and the extra information can come in handy later. But don't rush ahead to the back of the book - as the program has been written in the exact order you need to learn it. By the time you finish this book, you will thoroughly understand each technique and be ready to embark on your training program.

I will teach you everything you need to know - but the most important thing is to create a mental training program for you, and that is my major goal. This is what creates the most powerful performances in the pool.

That is when your part of the deal comes in - to stick to the program until the results begin to come through. And when the results begin to happen, you'll know about it! Everything in this book is not in the program however - it actually *includes far more information than is required* for your training program. It's designed to provide you with a great depth of knowledge for later on, so you can troubleshoot any other problems that you may come across in the future. This also allows you to *tailor* your training program as your needs change over time.

This program has brought huge improvement and many personal best times, and I have no doubt that you can experience great success using it too. This is why I have tried to keep the program as simple, easy and user-friendly as possible - it takes a very small amount of time each day to follow the program. All you have to do is be dedicated enough to use the program on a daily basis, and you should experience great improvement in your performance. So remember, all I can do is show you how, the rest is up to you.

Even though it only takes a small amount of time each day, many swimmers do not possess the kind of *long-term* dedication to keep it up, so you must discipline yourself to do the exercise (which by the way, is actually a lot of fun!). That is the only catch, but if you *really* want success badly enough, I'm sure you'll be fine.

There'll be many ideas in this book, which might create an impact on you immediately, and so the best thing to do is jot them down on paper immediately. This is because some of the most relevant information (to you, personally) may not always be listed in the summaries at the end of each chapter, but in some of the finer points I mention along the way, so best to jot them down as you go.

To Begin

Over the years I've worked with many swimmers of all levels from Sydney, Australia, plus I've been very lucky to be in contact with thousands of swimmers and coaches from all over the world through my website (www.swimpsychology.com) - and the one thing that I've noticed more than anything is that the vast majority do not seem to have any *real* inner belief in themselves and their ability.

This creates *other* problems during meets like severe nervousness, inconsistency, training great but racing badly, intimidation

Mind Training for Swimmers

from competitors, and so on. So in this book I have listed every technique, every mental secret required to overcome all these problems and more, plus help improve your times and create the results you desire. These techniques WORK. They've worked for many years and they will continue to bring results - even results that have surprised me! They must be used exactly as I say however, in order to 'fire on all cylinders'.

Mental training is now essential for any swimmer or athlete to make it to the elite level - it's one of the reasons why we are still continuing to produce new world records. This is because humans use *less than one percent* of their mind's capabilities! Yes, you've read correctly, less than one percent - but this is good news because it means that YOU are still capable of *huge* improvement! I doubt there would be a top athlete in the world today who doesn't use some form of mental training. It's used in all sports all over the world - but the interesting thing is, compared to other sports, it's been incredibly slow to happen in swimming. This is because, in my opinion, the majority of swimmers are only interested in *physical* training, and have no interest in mental training at all - yet mastering the mind is now becoming an *essential ingredient* to reach the elite levels of any sport.

Your Mind Is The Control-Centre Of *All* Movement!

One main thread that you will find throughout this book is this; your mind controls your body. Think about that for a moment. Your mind controls your body, NOT the other way around.

Mind Training for Swimmers

The swimmers who don't train their minds simply do not have great control over their *bodies* either! This leaves their performance open to *chance* every time they go out to race. That makes it a pretty important issue, wouldn't you think? Mental training may well be the vital difference between you attaining your dreams, or not - so do not take it lightly!

Training your mind is the same as training your body - it takes time to become mentally tough, so be prepared to put in some hard mental work if you want to get there. When two swimmers are of the same ability and similar training, it's the *mind* that determines the winner, so this will give you an advantage over other swimmers who don't have a mental training program.

The goal of this program is to help you to *pre-program* your swim before you go to the pool, and to overcome any problems or limitations that you may have been experiencing up until now. When you've completed this book, you will have the *knowledge* to get into a peak frame of mind before you go out to race in a meet.

Sorry, but the discipline will be up to you! So get ready to increase your mental and physical power, and over time you should find that your swimming will simply begin to improve effortlessly, but only on the condition that you use the mental training program on a regular daily basis.

As you know very well, it's only a very slight edge that separates a winner from the rest of the field. One second in swimming can be an eternity, and that is all it takes for a champion to show their superiority.

Mind Training for Swimmers

The mind is what creates this slight edge you're searching for. There was a time when only the world's champions did mental training, but now athletes all over the globe are realising that training their bodies *alone* will not get them to the top.

In the past, if a swimmer was racing badly, the first thing they'd do was train even *harder*. Sometimes this would pay off, but often it would lead to *over-training* - like a 19 year-old national swimmer I worked with, who discovered her energy levels were the same as that of a 50 year old!

Two main reasons caused many swimmers to turn to mental training. One was that many would swim unbelievable times in training but perform badly in the meets. The other was that most swimmers had also lost to competitors who simply *were not as good as they were* - and so it became obvious that the mind was the difference between winning and losing.

I'm sure you know deep down that you could be a better swimmer than you are right now - and that is why you are here. Possibly you're a swimmer who's put in the hard hours in training, but have not received the results that you deserve, and so you're making your first move into mental training. Or maybe you've done some form of mental training already, and are looking to further your knowledge. Either way, this book will contain everything you need.

It's a tragedy that in the past many fine swimmers have retired in frustration, not knowing that if only they'd trained their *minds* as well, they may have been champions. Mental toughness creates the ability to

Mind Training for Swimmers

pull a win out of even the most terrible circumstances, when you are not at your best.

The very fact that you're reading this book demonstrates that you are interested in attaining greater success, so let's begin your training, by first of all showing you how your mind and body are working when you are swimming at your best, and also the times when you are not. This knowledge is <u>essential</u>, so don't skip ahead, otherwise the rest of the book may not make any sense!

CHAPTER 2

The Magical Power Of Belief

If you believe you can win, you can - and if you believe you can't, you won't. It's that simple.

Probably the most important thing of all when you are racing is your own inner belief. Nothing can replace it, and you either have it, or you don't – there is no in-between. The swimmers who become successful always possess strong inner belief, because there is simply no way to succeed without it.

Let me tell you why. The mind's main *fuel* is belief (in yourself), and so it wouldn't matter if you could swim like Michael Phelps, because if you couldn't match his *level of belief*, you wouldn't be able to even go close to matching his results. The greatest swimmers of the era simply have no doubt in their mind that they are the best - *they simply do not question their ability.* (This is not to say they don't have to battle the usual worries and doubts that everyone else goes through leading up to a big event, they simply handle these better than most).

Mind Training for Swimmers

Of course, many don't often display this deep inner confidence, as sometimes this can just be inviting unwanted attention. They may appear to be a picture of complete modesty, but deep down, they know they are the best, and this is one of the main reasons why they *are*.

Back in 1954, when no athlete in the world had ever run a mile in under 4 minutes, it was claimed by doctors and other health professionals at the time that the human body was simply *not made* to accomplish such a feat. It was 'too much for the human body to handle', they claimed. The global belief was that the 4-minute mile was impossible, and this belief was proven correct because no one could break it.

Then suddenly Roger Bannister came along and blew away the record - and everyone's belief suddenly changed to, "Hey! It *is* possible!" And do you know what happened then? One month after Bannister set his record someone broke it. Then someone broke it again, and again, and during the 12 months after Bannister's record, 32 people broke the four-minute mile! And now, that 'impossible' time is now regularly run at school carnivals! That time is now considered to be a *joke* by today's world standards.

This has always been the case in swimming as well. Let's face it, most of today's world records will be considered *easy* in ten year's time! This is because today's standards will be generally *perceived* as well below the current standard of competition in ten year's time (with the exception of a few long-standing world records), and this belief is what determines the standard of performances.

Mind Training for Swimmers

So the question is, what do you consider impossible right now? What limits are you putting on yourself? Because whatever you consider to be impossible, will *probably be achieved* by someone one day. So why not you? Open up your mind to new possibilities, and see what really *is* possible.

Belief is what sets our limits upon ourselves. Here's an example of how powerful belief really is, in our everyday lives. A well-known doctor who worked with AIDS patients in the early 1980's said that the first 2 AIDS patients he ever had *recovered!* This was because at that stage the disease was unknown and had no name, and so his patients' belief systems told them that they would be fine - and they were. But this doctor said that once the virus hit the front page of the newspapers worldwide, saying this disease was 100% deadly, not one of his patients survived. This demonstrates the power of belief in our lives, and needless to say it also governs our swimming performances as well.

For instance, if you *believe* you can beat a certain competitor in a race, then this simply creates the *possibility* that you will win. It doesn't guarantee anything, but the *possibility is definitely there.*

However, if you *don't* believe that you can beat that particular competitor, there's absolutely *no possibility whatsoever* that you will beat that swimmer! This is how the power of belief totally rules your results in the pool.

This means that even if you're in a winning position, your mind can often *sabotage* your performance by causing you to lose rhythm or make a fundamental error at a crucial stage of the race. When this happens, of course, it *reinforces* the negative belief even further, making it an even harder pattern to break.

This is the power of the subconscious - your performance will *always* mirror the beliefs that you have about your swimming. This means that to move forward, often we must first *discover and then change our negative beliefs* to a more positive nature before our mind can generate great new performances in the pool. Let me explain.

Discover Your Own Hidden Beliefs

We all have *countless* beliefs – and about every subject you could possibly think of. In swimming alone, you have beliefs about how good you think you are, what you think you are able to achieve, and what you can't. You have beliefs about the swimmers you can beat, and those you cannot, the times you can achieve, and also those you think you can't.

This list goes on *ad infinitum* - you also have beliefs about all the different pools, equipment, training, coaches, competitors......you simply have *countless* beliefs, and this is only on the subject of swimming! You also have many beliefs about life in general - such as the music you like (and don't), the people you like (and don't!), school, work, religion, art, etc.

Our positive beliefs are vital to our chances of success in the pool, however the important thing for us to find out is what our *negative* beliefs are (about your swimming), as these are at the *core of what may be holding us back.* By overcoming our negative beliefs (and virtually

Mind Training for Swimmers

everyone has them) this can be like releasing weights from our legs and allowing you to bring our times down effortlessly.

So how do you find out what your beliefs are about your swimming? By looking for *patterns* in your performances - and asking yourself a few simple questions.

For instance, what limits have you reached, but have not been able to go any further? Who are the competitors that you can never seem to beat? What times have you set, but not been able to break through and go faster? Are there any mistakes that you tend to make over and over again? What pools do you swim badly in? These are clear ways of seeing where we harbour negative beliefs about our performance.

It is probably a good idea right now to jot down any negative areas you wish to improve - as these will be some of the areas we will be focusing our techniques on later.

Beliefs are very much like weeds in a garden, which we need to clear before we can get anything new to grow. Some have not been there long and can be pulled out easily, but others may have been there for years and must be tugged at for a while before they'll come out.

The good news is that if you have a long-term negative belief such as this, and even though it may have taken years to form, it generally takes only weeks or a few months to remove it.

In fact, changing your beliefs is much like using a video or DVD recorder - once you record a new television program over an old one, the old program is gone forever - and you're left with the new one. The same happens with beliefs - using the visualization and affirmation techniques

Mind Training for Swimmers

I'll show you shortly, you can simultaneously *erase* the negative beliefs forever and replace them with positive ones. Once you've done this, the sky's the limit!!

The Mirror Technique for Increasing Belief

Before I begin discussing the visualization technique, which is the main method and highly effective at *changing* beliefs (and also increasing self-belief) I'm going to show you another method called the Mirror Technique, which is also fabulous for increasing your inner belief.

Needless to say, there are several ways to increase your self-belief, including the visualization technique. The most common way for people to increase belief is to simply work hard, improve, and slowly gain better results, and this slowly increases your belief in yourself. However, this works for some, but not for others – and it also tends to be a rather slow and laborious way of doing things (I prefer much faster methods!).

Often a huge 'breakthrough' swim can give inner belief an enormous boost, or quantum leap forward – such as swimming a fabulous time or winning a big race. But of course, this is not always particularly easy to do either – that is, until you *have* the belief to power you along in your races.

Here is another technique, which I saw used by a martial arts class once, which involved each person staring into their own eyes in the

Mind Training for Swimmers

mirror, and speaking directly to their own subconscious mind. This was very, very powerful – give it a try.

This technique has proven to be a fabulous way of increasing your own levels of inner belief, yet strangely enough, the swimmers who most *need* the confidence are the very ones who are most uncomfortable doing this exercise! They often feel silly or embarrassed doing it, *even when they are on their own.* Yet I found that swimmers who *already have* a strong level of self-belief have no trouble doing it at all.

This method is so simple you will wonder how it can possibly have any affect upon your swimming - but have no doubt about this. This technique will bring a steady improvement to your confidence, self-esteem, inner belief, (and of course, your results), if you use it faithfully on a regular basis. Without this, of course, there are no guarantees!

Having said that, I will *not* be making this exercise a part of your 'mandatory' mental training program, as there will already be enough techniques for you to use initially - however if you feel the need to use this one, it would definitely be an added bonus.

This exercise has to be done in front of a mirror, and definitely requires a little privacy so that your friends and family don't think you're a little crazy! Possibly at a time when you are the only one at home is best.

So here we go. First of all, I want you to stand in front of a mirror, about 10 steps back from it. Now you look at your own reflection in the mirror, and you have to generate a very *strong, serious and powerful* look on your face, this is important as your mind must not

Mind Training for Swimmers

catch any hint of joking during this exercise - absolutely NO smiling allowed!

Now, I want you to stare at the reflection of your own eyes. At no time must you take your focus off them, not even for a moment, just continue to look deeper and deeper into them.

Now say aloud to yourself in a strong voice full of conviction, "I am power!". Now allow those words to sink in for a few seconds and feel their strength circulating through your body, whilst maintaining focus on the reflection of your eyes.

Now, take a step closer to the mirror - continuing to look into your eyes, and repeat it again with even more conviction - "I am POWER!" Once again allow these words and their power to wash over you.

Once again take another step closer to the mirror, maintaining the focus on your eyes, and once again, repeat "I am power!" Continue to do this until you're almost right up against the mirror - then repeat it twice more from close range, with great conviction - whilst staring directly into your own eyes from six inches away. Once you have done this, close your eyes, take a deep breath, and imagine your lungs filling with power, strength and confidence.

Feel this power flowing right through your body. As you exhale breathe out all *doubt, fear, worry and anxiety*, letting them go forever. Repeat this again, breathing in, and then breathing out.

This is the end of the exercise, which is incredibly effective if used with conviction and regularity - which are essential to make it work

Mind Training for Swimmers

properly. This method can also be used just before you leave home to race. Do not doubt the power of this technique. I've seen it work minor miracles with swimmers who had once been low in confidence. It is a direct line to the subconscious, which is what makes it so effective, and this is not easily achieved with other techniques.

I will go into more detail about how we *create* beliefs, (and later how to *change* them), in the next chapter on the mind/body relationship, which is vital to your improvement - however, before we move on to that, I want to show you yet another fabulous technique for creating powerful beliefs. This method is also not part of your mandatory Mental Training Program, but an additional technique that I am letting you know about if you decide you would like to include it into your own personal program.

The basis behind this method is that what you *believe* is more important than anything else, right before you are about to race. Of course, thoughts are important too, but your beliefs will actually have a major part in *determining your results* that day. So I am going to let you know what I regard to be the 5 most important beliefs to remember when you are approaching a meet. What you need to do is instil these into your mind and make them your *automatic* attitude to all meets from now on.

These beliefs can transform your performance without even changing a single thing in your training - they create *inner change*, which automatically creates the outer changes you, desire. But creating these beliefs is the hard work that I leave up to you - this is where your

Mind Training for Swimmers

discipline must come in, because I can't be there every minute of the day to keep you motivated to do it!

What you do is focus upon just one of these beliefs each week, and allow it to wash through your mind regularly throughout that entire week, by re-visiting the thought in your mind as often and regularly as you can throughout the day.

Then, the following week, focus upon the second belief, and then the third week on the third belief, and so on - until they become a normal part of your everyday belief system and mental attitude. If after 5 weeks you do not feel they have become part of your belief system, repeat this five-week process again until they are.

As soon as these begin to become your firm beliefs, you will begin to notice a major shift forward in your results - and the PB's (personal best times) will flow through much more easily.

Please note: Once again, while this is a very powerful practice, I have not included it as a *mandatory* part of your mental training program, as I am keeping the program as simple, powerful and straightforward as possible so that it is easy to follow. But if you wish to also add this exercise, then it certainly can only help! Now, these statements below are purely *thoughts* you need to *think* only - NOT to be *spoken* to others (you will soon see why).

Belief No. 1 - I Have No Limits

"I feel great today and there is *nothing* I can't do in the pool today. What's to stop me? Everybody look out!"

Mind Training for Swimmers

You must know that there is absolutely nothing to stop you putting in a great performance. Think of yourself as unlimited, unstoppable, unbeatable, supreme and all-powerful. This ensures that you do not get dragged into thinking about obstacles or other negatives, but see nothing but *opportunities* ahead for you.

Belief No. 2 - These Conditions Are Perfect For Me!

"These conditions are perfect for me today! There's water in the pool, heaps of competitors, and it's a great day for a win!"

Basically this means that it doesn't matter *what* the conditions are, you will succeed anyway. This must be your attitude, regardless of the conditions. Every day must be a perfect day to swim – in your mind - from now on. Don't let conditions get in the way of a great race or practice session. As soon as you begin criticizing the conditions, it is allowing your mind to dwell upon negative thoughts, and come up with excuses in case you do not put in a great performance – and ready-made excuses created before your swim are the absolute gong of death to your races!

Belief No. 3 - I've Done The Work, And I Believe In My Ability

"I deserve to win this race - I've done the work, put in the hours, and *somebody* has to win it - so why not me? I *know* I'm going to give this race a real shake, because I'm good enough to beat *any* of these people".

Mind Training for Swimmers

Know that you can achieve your goal. Why shouldn't you? You have done the work, you are doing mental training, you have given yourself every reason to be confident – and you have no idea whether your competitors have been as dedicated with their training as you have.

Belief No. 4 - Nothing Can Affect Me

"I'm a machine! Nothing can bother me or stop me today, not the swimmers, not the pool, my schedule, *nothing!* I'm completely in control of my own thoughts. I'm untouchable".

Never let anybody's comments or attitude get in your way - stay with your own positive thoughts, and surround yourself with positive people. Keep away from negative people as much as you can – however, if you can't manage to completely avoid them, ensure you do not allow anything they say to have the slightest affect upon your mental attitude. Regard yourself as being totally surrounded by a positive bubble of energy, which cannot be penetrated by anyone – especially by those who are only worried about trying to bring others down, instead of focusing upon their own swim.

Belief No. 5 - You Have Me To Worry About!

"These guys must be worried about me in this race - I'm going to be very tough to beat today!"

Don't waste your time worrying about your competitors - let them worry about you instead. Allow your mind to focus only upon positive things, leave it to your competitors to wallow in their doubts

Mind Training for Swimmers

and fears – and believe me, they have them. So disconnect from this 'normal' way of thinking and try the opposite – just focusing on your own race and letting all the others worry about you, instead.

These are the 5 beliefs that can transform your swimming – so if you wish to add this to your program, all you do is focus upon each belief for an entire week, before moving on to the next. Regard it as a type of '5 Week Challenge' if you like, and by the end of the 5 weeks, you should have these positive beliefs more firmly ingrained in your mind.

But once again, this technique is only optional, because I have some essential techniques coming up that are a mandatory part of your Mental Training Program, and so I have not added this exercise, as I do not want you to feel distracted from doing these essential techniques. However, it might be something worth considering later, once you have your program up and running. Here is your summary for this chapter, which at this stage does not contain any compulsory mental exercises for your Mental Training Program.

Summary

- Begin examining what it is you believe, and what you think is possible (and impossible). Write down any areas of your swimming where you think there may be a negative belief responsible, as you will want to focus upon improving these areas with the program. Begin to open your mind to new possibilities.

Mind Training for Swimmers

- Try the Mirror Technique - it boosts your self-confidence and inner belief.

- Keep the 5 Major Swim Beliefs in mind, and add them to your mental training program when you get the time.

Editor's Note: A recent self recognition study done on 12-15 month old children through UCSD (University of California, San Diego) contains data showing the spikes in their brain waves prove self-recognition when they look into a mirror. This leads one to the premise that how you view yourself is primal, and extremely important.

Mind Training for Swimmers

CHAPTER 3

It's Essential To Understand Your Mind/Body Relationship

It's time to truly begin your training - and the first step is to understand just what goes on between your mind and your body while you're swimming. The first thing you must know is that you actually have *two* minds. That's right, two minds - a conscious mind, and a subconscious mind.

Your conscious mind is your normal daily awareness. For instance, when you wake up in the morning and begin to think about what to do that day that is your conscious mind thinking those thoughts. It makes your plans and decisions, thinks through problems and organizes your life in general.

In fact, it's often who we *think* we are, but really, it's just our conscious mind, thinking heaps of thoughts. While you are awake, your conscious mind is constantly thinking thoughts all day long - in fact, every single day you think around 60,000 thoughts! Unfortunately for us, often a great amount of these thoughts are *negative*, and this is what affects your performance.

Mind Training for Swimmers

In fact, your conscious mind is probably responsible for most of your *worst* performances in the pool! It's may be quite common for your conscious mind to regularly think negative thoughts such as failure, doubt, fear, worry and anxiety - because most people do, whether you realise it or not, and they create major problems in swimming. These negative thoughts are transmitted from your conscious mind by electrical impulses to your subconscious, which sends these messages to your brain. Your brain sends the electrical messages which contact the various parts of your body which are required to swim your race - and ultimately these negative thoughts appear in your body's *performance* - in the form of extreme nervousness, lack of belief, inconsistency, etc.

Now we have the bad news out of the way. The *good* news is that you possess a highly powerful subconscious mind, which is generally responsible for your personal best times and greatest performances. So let's talk about how you can use it to improve your times.

Your Subconscious - The Master Key To Improvement

Your subconscious mind is the sleeping giant inside you. Most people aren't even aware of it, and often go their entire lives without even knowing it exists - but champions know it very, very well.

Your subconscious never sleeps, not even for a second. This is because, without you even knowing, it's co-ordinating countless functions every second, such as your heart beat, breathing, circulation,

Mind Training for Swimmers

elimination, and many other similar functions. So basically it's job is to keep you alive!

Your subconscious is your *inner intelligence*, which runs virtually every part of your life. You're never *consciously* aware of this because it all happens automatically – for instance, you don't have to *try* to breathe, or *make* your heart beat, it just happens automatically, and that is your subconscious at work. Your subconscious takes commands from your conscious mind, and obeys instructions without question. It doesn't matter whether the command is positive or negative, intelligent or stupid. It simply acts like a computer responding to your keyboard, no questions asked. This is why some days it will provide you with a great performance, and other days it won't - it all depends on what data has been *programmed* into it.

In fact, your subconscious is so computer-like in the way it operates, here's an interesting fact about it; if right now you vividly imagined in your mind that you were swimming, your subconscious would actually send the very *same* electrical impulses to your brain that it would send if you really *were* swimming! This means that it literally can't tell the difference between reality and something vividly imagined, and for that moment, it would believe that you were actually in the pool. This is a very valuable piece of information, which we will be using to your advantage a little later.

So to recap, when you're on the block ready to dive into the pool, it's your conscious mind which sends the command, and then it's your subconscious that acts on this command, sending electrical impulses to

Mind Training for Swimmers

your brain, which sends messages off to your arms, legs and body - and splash, you've dived in! This is how it all works. Even to move one single step, this incredible process must happen in order to simply move your foot.

As your conscious mind is generally responsible for your *worst* performances in the pool, what you need to do is learn to override your conscious mind and use your subconscious more effectively.

The Place You Store Your Swimming Experiences

An amazing facet of the subconscious is its incredible memory bank, where you keep all your swimming *experiences* stored. For instance, whenever you've trained, or swum at a meet, your subconscious has taken a perfect copy of every single action, every single stroke, your stroking rhythm, even every *thought* that you had on those days, and stored it all into your memory bank.

This memory bank has records of every event that has ever happened in your entire life. That's right, your subconscious mind, under hypnosis, could tell you what colour socks you wore on your 3rd birthday, or the colour of the clothes your parents were wearing on your 4th birthday!

Every life event is stored in there, but more importantly for you, you use this incredible memory bank to store away all your swimming experiences, and you draw on these memories every single time you go to the pool. There you may swim a great time, and then *that* swim experience is also added to your collection of memories, which allow

Mind Training for Swimmers

you to improve even further. This is how all humans improve, we remember our past experiences, and the knowledge we learned from them, and then we improve upon them further, and store away the new experiences and knowledge for use at a future time.

So this means that, right now, within your subconscious is the blueprint for the absolute *perfect swim!* This is because in the past, from the many thousands of strokes you'd have swum, you would probably have swum at least *one* perfect stroke. When you have achieved anything even *once*, your subconscious can *repeat it again and again.* This is one of the main aspects you will use to bring out your best performances in the pool.

Your subconscious simply knows exactly how to swim the perfect lap or race - it's just that very few of us trust it enough to use it. It's much like having a brand new Ferrari in your garage, but saying "I'm not sure if I trust that car, I'll take the bus instead"!

The fact is that every time you've swum your best times, it was your *subconscious, which* was responsible for your performance, with barely a ripple of interruption from your conscious mind. Unfortunately it's not often allowed to do this, by the dominating conscious mind.

The two things that mainly prevent great times in the pool are:

- Either the conscious mind takes complete control of your performance in the pool (which it handles very poorly); or

Mind Training for Swimmers

- It often programs your subconscious with fears, worries, doubts and anxieties that will badly affect performance.

If these negative thoughts occur regularly, they become a part of your *everyday thinking*, and this creates powerful negative beliefs within your subconscious – which, as you know, are bad news! So the conscious mind can sabotage your success in either of these two ways. However, we'll shortly be discussing the number one subject of this book - how to *override* the conscious mind and allow your subconscious to take control of your swimming – in fact, let's start right now.

CHAPTER 4

Transform Your Times Using Visualization

Let's now begin discussing the techniques that you can use to overcome negative beliefs, and also to *pre-program* your swim before you go to the pool. These techniques can also help you to overcome nagging problems that may have plagued you for years, such as nervousness, lack of consistency, intimidation, or not having enough self-confidence.

These techniques have turned around many swimmers' performances. One swimmer I worked with had been out of training for many months due to a long illness, yet after a couple of practice sessions he swam a personal best time, simply from using these techniques. I still remember how amazed he was, saying that if he'd been in full training, he would have swum even faster. I'm not saying that if you were sick and out of training for months that this would happen to you, but it illustrates what is actually *possible* through the power of your mind.

Mind Training for Swimmers

"I tried to picture a black Ferrari. I tried to think of a car and just shift into gears – first gear on the first lap, second gear on the second lap, third gear on the third lap and fifth gear on the way back. It obviously worked."

Leisl Jones – Gold Medallist Athens 2004 Olympics

Mind Training for Swimmers

Visualization

The first technique is visualization, which is probably the most powerful technique available to improve your performance and times. It's used by virtually every world-class swimmer, athlete or sports person in the world, because it's highly effective, easy to use, and can overcome any number of sports-related problems.

Visualization is using your very powerful imagination, to picture in your mind the exact way you would like to swim at a certain meet. It's often called *mental rehearsal*, because what you're doing is rehearsing the swim in your mind, which sets up a blueprint for your body to follow. On the day of the meet, your body simply follows those instructions automatically.

Regardless of what areas you need to work on, this technique can help you get the results you want. Before I go more in-depth about visualization, there is one condition, which must be abided if you want to get great results from this technique. Visualization only takes about 8-15 minutes, but it will not work effectively unless it's used virtually each and every day. That's right, every day, only for about 8-15 minutes, but every single day.

If you use this technique every second or third day, you simply won't get the results you want. Don't worry, the time invested will be worth it, and even though it may seem like a chore, it actually is a lot of fun and relaxation - my clients usually find (much to their surprise) the begin *rushing home* from school or work just to do this technique!

Mind Training for Swimmers

So before we go any further, you must vow to yourself that you have the dedication and the discipline to use this technique every single day. It only takes a short time, but you'd be amazed at how few people can manage to keep it up for even a month! This is the difference between being the best, or the rest.

What Can Visualization Do For You?

It can:

- *Program* your body for a perfect swim
- Overcome long-term recurring problems and negative beliefs
- Prevent unnecessary mistakes
- Help you to maintain your focus
- Improves rhythm
- Helps overcome technical problems
- Overcomes nervousness
- Builds confidence and inner belief
- Learn new skills quicker - eg. kicks, turns
- Can assist you to overcome injuries and even sickness in quicker time.

I believe there are simply no other mental techniques that can influence performance with the same ease and effectiveness as visualization. It's easy and doesn't take much time, and so it's not only effective but also convenient to fit in with your daily life.

Mind Training for Swimmers

So all you have to do, each and every day of the week, is put aside 10-15 minutes of your time to program your mind with success, by imagining the perfect swim in your mind. This sets up a blueprint in your subconscious for your body to follow, and I will show you how to do this shortly.

Don't be fooled by how simple this sounds - in my opinion there is not a technique in the world that can match it for improving performance. There are very few, if any, world-class athletes in *any* sport who don't use some form of visualization, simply because it creates a massive advantage for those who use it.

The visualization technique almost sounds a little *too* simple to be as incredibly effective as it is, and believe it or not, you've already been using visualization every day of your life! You see, every single thought you've ever had in your life has created an *image* (or picture) within your subconscious - so really, visualization is something you are constantly using.

For instance, right now if you think of your car, your house, or your best friend, each time you will find that a picture or an image of them appears in your mind. This is visualization - it's simply *pictures running through your mind*.

The only problem with this is, often before races, I find that many swimmers choose to run *horror movies* through their minds - of either terrible swims they've had in the past, or of the terrible swim they expect to swim in a moment - literally programming themselves to fail. Needless to say - to swim badly, this works really effectively!

Mind Training for Swimmers

This form of 'negative' visualization can create *mental blocks* that need to be overcome before they may be able to improve any further. Swimmers who run these swim horror movies regularly through their minds often reach a point of *stagnation* in their swimming career, where they simply seem to stop improving altogether. Their swimming reaches a complete standstill and refuses to improve any further, no matter how hard they train. This is definitely the time to use mental training – and I find that most swimmers contact me when they have reached this stage!

So we must be really careful what we think - your subconscious simply accepts whatever thoughts are put into it, and so it will act on negative suggestions just as easily as positive ones. This is actually great news, because from today you're going to begin feeding positive information into your subconscious!

Some Tricks To Visualization

Let's discuss some of the important elements essential to visualize successfully. First of all, it's really important before you begin the visualization exercise to make sure you won't be interrupted by noise such as phones or other people. The reason for this is because you're going to temporarily go into the make-believe world of your subconscious - and interruptions from the outside world do not help this process.

What you are trying to do is literally fool your subconscious into believing that instead of sitting in a chair with your eyes closed, you're

Mind Training for Swimmers

actually in a pool, swimming the perfect race – and you do this by vividly imagining this scenario on the screen of your mind. Which means that it's highly important that outside noises are prevented from interrupted your daily 'programming'.

Another reason for being free of interruptions is because when you visualize, you need to be in a state of *light relaxation*, and it's quite amazing just how loud a telephone can sound when you happen to be in a relaxed state!

So before you begin, always make sure the phones are turned off, and that no one is going to come into the room and interrupt you. Being in a relaxed state helps to shut down the incessant chatter of your conscious mind, and this allows the exercise to make a more powerful impression upon your subconscious. I will go into a little more detail about the relaxation in the step-by-step explanation later.

Once you're relaxed, it's then time to begin creating movies in your mind, with yourself being the star of the movie. You can do this in several ways. One method is where you visualize yourself doing everything in the *correct order* it would normally happen, such as arriving at the pool, being in the marshalling area, then being on the block ready to go, followed by the dive, the swim, the result and maybe the celebration with your friends or family. This is one method which works very well, but some prefer another method which is less structured, such as the free flowing method.

The free flowing method is where you simply allow the images to *run freely through your mind* in any particular order that feels

Mind Training for Swimmers

comfortable. There is no real organization of the images, your mind is simply allowed to focus upon whatever part of the swim it wishes to, and some find this is a very relaxed approach.

Either of these methods are equally effective - you can use either one, or even mix the two together a little if you wish. It's your movie, you're the director (and also the star) so you can literally create it any way you want.

It doesn't matter if you can't get perfect colour pictures in your mind when you visualize, so never worry about this. Your subconscious knows exactly what you're trying to imagine. In fact, it's not so much the pictures that are important, as much as the *feelings* that you inject into your visualizations. When you add powerful feelings to the images you're creating, it makes a much deeper impression on your subconscious. So when you're imagining yourself swimming unbelievably well, create feelings of excitement, happiness, strength and power, of being unbeatable!

For instance, when you're in a cinema watching a movie, you don't sit there and say to yourself "this isn't real, this is just a screen and a projector, I can't get into this", because to really enjoy the movie, you willingly suspend your disbelief for a while and just immerse yourself in the movie. In fact, you virtually put yourself *in* the movie, and once you do this, you get emotionally involved in it and really enjoy it. This is exactly the approach you need with your mental programming - you go into your own inner world and create this life-like movie about yourself, including the *feelings* of being a winner. This sends clear messages to

Mind Training for Swimmers

your subconscious, which it can act upon immediately. This is one of the most essential ingredients for success.

More Important Ingredients

When you visualize, feel free to use some *creativity* in this movie you're making. The main way to do this is using imagery. For instance, after I take a swimmer through a race visualization, I will often taken them through another quick 'race' where they imagine their body becoming a torpedo or a dolphin as soon as they hit the water, and they imagine themselves cruising through the water at amazing speed, leaving everyone way behind. Imagery sends strong messages through to your subconscious and works very well - more on this later.

The only other vital things to remember when using the visualization technique is to keep all images both positive, and also present tense.

When I say that the visualization must be positive, this means to always imagine yourself succeeding, not failing! It's amazing how many people imagine losing, or making errors, in their mind - and as I said before, it works very effectively! You must always win the races in your mind, and the easier, the better. And always see an error-free swim – the perfect swim, every time. Never, ever visualize a negative result - if you do, mentally cross it out and visualize it over again.

When I mentioned that your images must be in the *present-tense*, I mean that if you're 'programming' yourself for a future meet in a month's time, never imagine it actually *being* in the future, always

Mind Training for Swimmers

visualize it as if it's already happening *right here and now*. Your subconscious has no actual concept of time, so if you set your goals into the future, that is where they'll stay, in the future! This means they'd never arrive in the here and now, which is not what you want.

So even if you're visualizing for the Olympics, swim that Olympic race every single day in your mind as if it's happening right here and now. By the time you're at the Olympics you will have already swum that race a thousand times!

Also, it's fine to visualize several different *events* from your next meet during your visualization, but probably a maximum of three events. You want your mind to focus upon just a few *particular* goals or events, rather than spreading its attention over too many different events.

This brings us to the *most essential ingredient* for successful visualization, which is to visualize regularly. For instance, it's better to visualize for 10 minutes each day, than for 2 hours, 3 days a week.

Just imagine your mind as an Olympic swimming pool (which should not be difficult!) and each day you put 2 or 3 drops of red ink into the pool. For a few days or weeks you may see no change at all in the colour of the pool, however in a couple of months you will have a completely red pool! This is certain, and so even though the change is very slow and gradual, it absolutely must happen, eventually.

This is exactly how your mind works - with gradual change. If you visualize each day for 10-15 minutes, being patient for the results without expecting miracles overnight, then you should vastly improve

Mind Training for Swimmers

your times in the pool. I can honestly say that I have never seen this technique *not* help any kind of sporting performance, when it is used correctly.

It can also be quite effective to supplement your main daily visualization with occasional short 5-30 second 'flashes' of the event through your mind. These can be done during your *normal awakened* state, either with your eyes open or closed, and they do not require any relaxation – it is purely a super-quick replay of the race you have been visualizing. These mental 'flashes' will certainly not *replace* the daily exercise, but can help to refresh or top-up your mental training during the day whenever you have a spare moment.

Needless to say, during the 2 weeks before a meet, an extra full-visualization session will also be helpful if you have time on a particular day. However, if not, try using the 'flash' method.

Schedule Your Mental Training

The most important thing about visualization is that you DO it! The key to this is to schedule a time in your day, which is convenient for you to do the visualization exercise. Swimmers are generally busy people who fit swimming training into the rest of their daily timetable, and so it's essential to *schedule your visualization* into your day as well, so it doesn't get dropped off the priority list.

Is early morning best for you, or when you get back from morning training? Or do possibly afternoons, early evening or even just before bedtime suit you better? Decide on your best time and try to

Mind Training for Swimmers

maintain your daily visualization session. If the only way you can manage it is with a *different time each day*, then schedule it before each day begins, it is vital you do not sacrifice it for other things. It is not an hour we are talking about, it is just 10-15 minutes - that's all. Make sure you give it priority if you are serious about using mental training and getting some results from it.

As I mentioned earlier, this exercise can actually become a huge bonus in your life, outside of the great results you can attain from it for your swimming. I often noticed that when I'd first mentioned the daily visualization to a swimmer, they'd often groan "oh no, not *every* day!" Yet by the time I'd see them a month later, I'd find out that they'd often *hurried home from school or work* just to do the exercise, because it had become such a fabulously relaxing part of their day which they did not want to miss!

You see, visualization has so many *additional* benefits attached to it, I could not fit them all into this book. For instance, a mother emailed me some time ago to say that her ten-year-old daughter had been using my visualization CD and that she had experienced remarkable improvements in her times. However, that was not why she was emailing – apparently these improvements were not restricted to her swimming, but, to their great surprise, they included several other areas of her life as well.

Not only had she shown a marked improvement in her swim times, she had also noticed huge improvements in her mathematics, memory, and overall confidence and positive attitude. These changes

Mind Training for Swimmers

had been so major that many people were asking what she was doing differently, and apparently even her doctor asked for my website address!

The relaxation factor alone is highly beneficial to your health, as well as the increased abilities to concentrate, think clearly, feel more positive and be in emotional control - and this is why swimmers often report other improvements from their everyday life (again, much to their surprise).

Patience Brings Success

Something to beware is that many people *give up* on their mental training after just a few weeks, because they don't always see results *immediately*. Sadly many swimmers who are on the very brink of huge improvement do not persevere long enough to ever find out.

Mental training simply doesn't work this way. For instance, you never gave up swimming in the first few weeks because you couldn't swim Olympic times, did you?! The same goes with mental training, you get better the more you *practice*. It's like going to the 'inner gym' every day, which builds and strengthens your mental muscles. Even the visualization gets easier (and stronger) with each day you use it - because just like any exercise, it builds power the longer you do it.

If you can keep the visualization up for 6 weeks, you will have created a routine and will often have achieved some great results already in this time (otherwise you should be very close).

Mind Training for Swimmers

So set yourself a target of visualizing every day for the first 42 days. By this time you should be in a routine, and your subconscious should have become conditioned to the images you are putting into it. After this period, you can (if you wish) reduce your visualization time down to 8-12 minutes per day, as the subconscious program that has been created only needs to be *maintained and strengthened* after this period.

The key is to make your mental training become a part of your everyday routine, just like your physical training. Remember, champions leave nothing to chance, they train themselves physically *and* mentally.

Once again, never doubt the power of this technique, visualization is used all over the world - not only in swimming but all sports, as well as in the health industry, business and success training. It's recognized as one of the leading transformational techniques in the world today. If you have any doubts, just type the word into any search engine and you will see tens of millions of websites appear on the subject (which I just tested myself, and received 55 and a half million results!).

Another of its benefits is to help overcome extreme nervousness. If you ever feel so nervous that you think it will badly affect your race, then a special version of the 'sanctuary' method may be very helpful for you (I'll talk more about this shortly). Not all nervousness is bad, however, it's often a sign that you're psyched up and ready to go. So don't worry if you're nervous!!! This special version of the sanctuary

Mind Training for Swimmers

method is used purely for *extreme* nervousness. I remember having one swimmer who was so nervous, she would literally vomit before each race. Now *that's* extreme nervousness! Luckily this technique helped her considerably.

Music And Visualization

Something that I highly recommend you try is using *music* during your visualization - because it can help you to *feel* the emotions much more easily.

This of course, charges your images with an additional boost of power. You can actually create your own *personal visualization audio program*, by firstly recording a slow relaxing song, followed by two or three stirring, uplifting songs (all of your choice) onto a CD, or your iPod.

The first song is purely designed to get you into a nice relaxed state before the more upbeat, motivational songs come in, which are meant to inspire you and make you feel like a winner while you are visualizing powerful images of success in the pool. These songs should be changed regularly so that you do not become overly familiar with them - they must continue to have an emotional impact on you, and this can wear off if you use the same songs for too long.

Having this music visualization program can be very handy, not only at home but also *before race*s, because you can use an iPod Discman to program your mind for success right there at the pool, even if only for a few minutes. This is also great way of overcoming the

Mind Training for Swimmers

tension in the marshalling area, and programming your race for success before you begin. I will discuss music and visualization further shortly, when I take you step-by-step through the exercise.

For those interested, I have also created a Mind Training for Swimmers Daily Visualization Exercise on CD. It contains a visualization exercise, and additional features such as powerful *hypnotic suggestions*, which help to create effortless change, and also automatic relaxation, which is often the stumbling block for many people using visualization, as well as a guided race visualization. All that plus 45 minutes of information - for more information on this, go to the website www.swimpsychology.com and look for the link to the CD.

Vary Your Visualizations

Generally it's best to concentrate your visualization exercise on the next approaching meet - imagining the race at that particular pool and surroundings. However, there may be times when this may begin to become a little too *familiar* or even boring, similar to watching the same movie over and over again, and so some variation often can help this.

Here are some examples of how to bring some variation into a normal race visualization exercise (please note that some of these examples may be suitable mainly for up-and-coming swimmers rather than Masters swimmers, however older swimmers can simply insert a different scenario in its place). These are just some variations you may wish to try - you may not feel the need to use these, or you may have some ideas of your own.

Mind Training for Swimmers

Here are some ideas for variation in your visualizations:

- Changing the music on your personal visualization CD / iPod.

- *Alternating* music regularly for your visualization.

- Changing the location of your imagined swim to another pool.

- Changing the competitors in the imagined race.

- Imagine yourself as being a top international swimmer you greatly admire (this also works effectively for those who cannot visualize *their own bodies* very clearly).

- Imagining yourself winning major events - such as the Olympics, Pan Pacs etc. This can be fun, create some variation, and still 'program' a powerful performance into your subconscious.

- See yourself giving a press conference or interview after a great race, answering questions confidently, and photographers taking shots, etc.

- See your name written up in the newspaper, describing a brilliant swim of yours (otherwise seeing the swim in the swimming results column in the sport section).

- Remember and visualize all of your greatest swims from past performances.

Varying the visualization will ensure you won't get too familiar with the exercise, whilst changing the songs when they begin to become

Mind Training for Swimmers

too familiar is also highly recommended, in order to keep the exercise fresh and interesting. Let's now go into the basic mechanics of the exercise, so you'll know exactly what to do.

Visualization Explained Step-By-Step
Beginning Your Visualization

I will now discuss how to use the daily visualization exercise, so that you will be able to use the technique *both with and without* music. The segments to visualization include the initial relaxation, the race visualization, an imagery visualization, and last of all, coming out of the relaxation.

The initial relaxation is an essential part of the visualization exercise, as your subconscious simply will not take any notice of the images you are visualizing unless you are in a relaxed state. Without relaxation, there are far too many thoughts going on for it to focus properly – as your conscious mind chatters incessantly and bombards the subconscious with mindless drivel, preventing it from focusing upon the images you are trying to visualize.

Most swimmers find the relaxation the most difficult part of the whole exercise. Many report that they simply cannot get their minds to switch off. This is simply a case of trial and error, and conditioning your conscious mind to behave, which of course, is the last thing it wants to do!

Practice the relaxation in various ways (and I will suggest several in a moment), and endeavour to find the method that works best for you. This is a very crucial key to visualization - many swimmers visualize *perfectly* but get no results, because they simply cannot get their mind to drop down to a decent level of relaxation, and this means that the subconscious mind will not accept the images you are visualizing.

Here are some methods for improving your relaxation level before you move into the swim phase of the visualization exercise.

One option is to visualize first thing in the morning after you wake up - however this is probably only possible for those who do not have early morning training. For the first 15-20 minutes after you wake up, your mind is *naturally in a perfectly relaxed state* and will not require any relaxation exercises whatsoever - you simply begin visualizing your races immediately.

A good way to do this is to wake up to a clock radio (if you have one). Turn off the alarm by pressing the 'snooze' button, as this will allow you nine minutes or so to visualize in bed before the alarm goes off again, and you can then arise and go on with your day.

The only problem with this is that often you may find you will simply go straight back to sleep - and if this happens, you may have to sit up in bed to visualize your races.

If you do not have time to visualize in the mornings, this means you will need to use relaxation techniques to get your mind into the perfect state for visualization. This is where you find a quiet place where you can be away from people interrupting you, and you begin the

Mind Training for Swimmers

relaxation phase by closing your eyes and taking two or three slow, deep breaths.

If you decide to use your own music CD or music on iPod, this relaxation phase (and including the sanctuary phase, which I am about to explain) is used during the *first song* on your self-made compilation of songs – and this is a slow, relaxing tune designed purely for relaxation, nothing else. For this you can also use rainforest, dolphin or whale music if you prefer, which you often find in the relaxation section of music stores.

During this initial relaxation song, count backwards from 20 with each outbreath, all the way down to zero. This will take you into the first stages of light relaxation, and brings you up the sanctuary phase of the relaxation.

Find Your Sanctuary

The sanctuary is a 'place' you go to in your mind, to escape the world for a few minutes - it's a form of meditation that won't relax you *too much or too little*. This place is usually a different location for everyone. For some it might be a beach, for others it might be a rainforest or an island - it doesn't matter where you go in your mind as long as it's relaxing for you. You can also regularly change the location of your sanctuary if you wish, or you may wish to stay in the same location every time, it's totally up to you.

Being in your sanctuary is an extremely pleasurable experience, and you often may not want to leave it, to visualize your races! This is

Mind Training for Swimmers

why the sanctuary is also a fabulous pre-race relaxer for those who experience extreme nervousness before races, which I will discuss in a moment.

When you go to your sanctuary, it's important to make the images *realistic* so your mind can relax properly. This means it's best to use all your senses – that is, *see* the colours of the surroundings, *hear* the sounds in this place, *feel* the sensations of the sun on your back or a light breeze. If your imagination is exceedingly well developed, you might even be able to smell the aroma of this scene as well!

You only need to remain in your sanctuary for 2-4 minutes, before moving on to the swim phase of your visualization. Of course, when you are at the pool, it can be much more difficult to find a place quiet enough to do the visualization exercise, and so if possible, it's best to visualize before you leave home to go to the pool. However, whilst you are at the pool, you may wish to go out and sit in the quiet of your car, if you have one outside in the carpark (but make sure you have plenty of time before your race, and that you don't go to sleep!).

Otherwise you can simply pretend to have a nap in your seat, or put your Discman on and listen to your self-made musical visualization CD. Often people will not interrupt you if you have your eyes closed and have headphones on, and the headphones or earpieces also help to keep out some of the surrounding noise, which is also helpful.

Mind Training for Swimmers

An Extra Note -

Using The 'Sanctuary' For Nervousness Before Races

Before I move onto the swim phase of the daily visualization, I want to mention how you can also use your sanctuary to overcome extreme nerves before races.

If you find that you happen to suffer from *extreme* nerves before races, you can use the sanctuary technique for up to ten minutes, to calm down your emotions and take the edge off your nerves. Please note there is NO swim visualization involved with this, you simply go straight into your sanctuary, remain there for 10 minutes (no longer), and then come back out of your sanctuary by opening your eyes.

Whilst you are in your sanctuary, imagine that you have *all the time in the world* to be in this place - do not *clock watch* while you do the exercise, or it will distract you and prevent you from relaxing properly. You will generally know when you are around the ten-minute mark to finish - even though you may not want to! Otherwise you can either set your watch or mobile phone to set off an alarm in ten minutes, or ask someone to give you a nudge to let you know it's time to come back to the real world (make sure it's only a nudge though, not a punch!).

This method is a perfect relaxer as there are no images of races whatsoever, and doing this for 10 minutes reduces your stress levels without affecting your motivation or fighting spirit. After all, we don't want you feeling so at peace with the world that you don't care if you win or not!

Mind Training for Swimmers

Remember, however, that a little nervousness is absolutely fine - it's only the *extreme* nervousness that can affect your performance, and that can be removed by going to your sanctuary. The peace and clarity of thought that you receive from this method will remain for several hours, after which you can always go back to do it again, if needed. This is one of the best techniques for overcoming stress, anxiety and nerves. Now, onto to the swim phase of your daily visualization exercise.

Of course, last but not least, if you find that relaxation is a continuing problem during your visualizations, and that none of these ideas seem to work for you, try the visualization CD at my website – www.swimpsychology.com

The Swim Visualization

Once you have relaxed in your sanctuary for a few minutes, it is time to begin the swim phase of your visualization. If you are using a self-made music CD or iPod for your visualization, the first (relaxing) song is used for your *sanctuary*, and then from this point onward you visualize yourself winning races to *upbeat, motivational-sounding songs*.

When this upbeat song begins, you begin the swim visualization by imagining yourself at the pool, seeing the people that would normally be there (eg. your family / friends / coach), hearing all the usual *sounds* of a swim meet, and even smelling the chlorine of the pool – use all your senses and make it all as realistic as possible.

Mind Training for Swimmers

By the way, when you are visualizing, it *doesn't matter* if you are viewing each scene from *inside* your body, or looking down at yourself from *up above* - either method is fine, and whichever feels more natural to you is the better way to go.

Next you imagine yourself on the block, getting ready to begin your race, feeling strong and confident. Then when the race starts, see (*and feel*) your perfect dive, followed by powerful rhythmic strokes. From then on you simply imagine the race going *absolutely perfectly* in every way, seeing yourself moving ahead of the others, feeling absolutely fabulous and with heaps of energy.

Finally, you imagine yourself win the race by a good margin, and also *seeing the great time that you have recorded* – and follow this by allowing the feelings of joy, relief and excitement to wash right through your body, as if you had really won the race. This is very important, as it adds some powerful authenticity to the images. Imagine yourself being congratulated by family or friends, and make sure you really enjoy and *get into* this part of the exercise – so that you *feel* the joy and happiness of being the winner, who has swum a great time. Savour this feeling for a moment, before moving onto the next phase.

Finish With A Customized Imagery Visualization

After this race visualization, you swim one more race in your mind before you finish the exercise, and this part of the visualization utilizes very powerful *imagery*, which I will explain to you later (once I've shown you how to do it).

Mind Training for Swimmers

To do this, once again imagine yourself on the block, but this time, when you dive in and hit the water, you are going to visualize your body *transforming into a dolphin, torpedo* or anything else you can think of that is amazingly fast and totally unbeatable in the water - hurtling through the water at ridiculous speed, and literally leaving the rest of the field way, way behind. (Yes, I know this part of the visualization probably sounds strange, but hang in there and I will shortly explain why it is so powerful to do this).

When you visualize this segment, don't be conservative - see yourself lapping your competitors and absolutely leaving them for dead! To get the best out of this visualization, you must create the feeling of the incredible *raw power* the dolphin or torpedo generates in the water, and seeing just how totally dominant you are over the competition - know you simply *cannot be stopped* and are supremely unbeatable in this race.

When you use this visualization, often-fabulous feelings of strength, confidence and power flow through your mind and body, which is actually what makes it so effective. You may also have to imagine the pool being much *longer*, or even create additional laps for this visualization, otherwise the race would be all over in 2 seconds flat!

To finish this race in your mind, see yourself accelerate even faster to finish the race in spectacular style, but always *imagine your normal body return* as you win the race - followed by all the fabulous feelings of victory, and of being congratulated, all of which were at the finish of your first race visualization.

Mind Training for Swimmers

Once you have done this, you are finished. Then you simply allow yourself to slowly come out of the relaxed state - taking some deep breaths, slowly beginning to move your feet around a little, and when you're ready, opening your eyes - but take your time with this, don't rush this process or you may end up feeling a little dizzy or 'woozy'.

These are the basics of visualization for swimming, but there are many additional methods you can use with this technique for different purposes, and most, like the dolphin / torpedo visualization, use imagery to achieve the results.

Imagery In Your Visualizations

Imagery provides an added boost of jet propulsion to your daily visualization, as it utilizes the natural language of your subconscious mind (symbolism), which you may often notice is also present in your dreams every night during sleep. Using the natural language of your subconscious is another way of effectively programming your mind for success.

For instance, the dolphin / torpedo visualization sends a clear message to the subconscious along the lines of "I'm unbelievably fast, and totally unbeatable in the water". This of course, can only be good - because it means that your subconscious mind (which controls your co-ordination and movement) will send signals to your body designed to enable it to move very fast through the water.

Mind Training for Swimmers

Please note that you never have to worry about your subconscious mind attempting to copy the movement of a dolphin or torpedo as you swim, as the only true *reference points* your mind has for swimming are the *strokes you have programmed into it* from your countless training sessions. It will simply take the 'power and speed' message you have visualized, and apply it to your swimming. This is how imagery works, and it's very powerful.

Here are several other suggestions and ideas using imagery you might wish to consider during your visualizations, at times when it suits you:

Imagery For Power and Energy

During your visualization, when you see yourself on the block and about to start a race, imagine that your lane (and your lane *only*) is completely illuminated, or lit up, with incredibly vibrant *light and energy*. Then see this light and energy begin to extend up so that it radiates into your feet, and then upwards through your body - vibrating enormous power and energy through every atom of your body. *Feel* the warmth of this energy as it glows through your body, and *know* that this energy radiating through your lane and body will provide you with extra power and the vital *edge* over your competitors.

This was a technique used by an Olympic runner which I've adapted to swimming, which I've found works very easily and effectively for swimmers, and can even be used successfully for managing extreme swimming pain.

Mind Training for Swimmers

Method 1: Using Imagery For Overcoming Intimidation From Another Swimmer

These two visualization exercises are specialised for intimidation problems. Here's the first one:

Imagine in your mind the particular swimmer that you find intimidating, except rather than see them as they normally are, mentally *reduce them in size* - to appear much smaller, weaker and slower, and so that they no longer look at all intimidating.

Then, in comparison, imagine your own body, but exaggerate it somewhat so that it looks even stronger, faster and more powerful than normal. Finally, finish by reversing the old situation completely by imagining that *they* are now intimidated by you, and feel the power of knowing that you are the one who is now in control. This helps to reverse the subconscious fear, which has built up concerning that particular swimmer, as this visualization acts on the very source of the fear, within the subconscious.

Do this regularly, and soon you will never worry about that swimmer again! Also see the next visualization in Method 2, which can also be used for intimidation.

Mind Training for Swimmers

Method 2: Using Imagery For Overcoming Intimidation From Another Swimmer

The best way to describe this technique is to explain how one of my clients used it to great affect to overcome his own intimidation problems. He was a sixteen-year-old National level swimmer (who we shall call Matt), who had not beaten a particular competitor for four years straight. Matt had a major mental block about this, to the point where, even when he was way ahead of his competitor in a race, his mind would sabotage his performance. He would begin to make some uncharacteristic and incredibly simple mistakes (for a swimmer of his level) or begin to lose his stroking rhythm during the latter part of the race, and of course, he would end up losing the race to his competitor – once again.

Needless to say, each time Matt would lose the race to his archrival, the negative belief causing all the problems became *even more* firmly entrenched, ingrained and powerful. Matt was getting into an ever-deepening rut every time he competed against him, and he could not get out of it.

So, when Matt came to see me, I first of all tried to get Matt to simply visualize beating this rival, using the traditional visualization technique. To my surprise, this didn't work at all, as by this time Matt was so scared and psyched out by his competitor, his mind literally 'froze' every time he tried to even picture this guy! It was similar to the way a mouse *freezes* in fear when it sees a snake - just like on those wildlife television shows or Discovery channel!

Mind Training for Swimmers

So then I decided to apply some imagery to the situation instead, and I asked Matt what his favourite animal was. Matt gave me a pretty strange look at first, but then replied that his favourite animal was a rabbit. So with this information, I told Matt that the next time he visualized his competitor, I wanted him to see his competitor's face as being that of a rabbit - complete with big ears, long teeth and whiskers.

Needless to say, Matt thought I had completely 'lost it' by this stage (and I am sure he was wondering why his mother had brought him to see this crazy therapist) but, despite that, I still managed to make him promise to do this, in his daily visualization for the following three weeks. We would soon find out how well the technique worked, because he was to compete against his archrival at a meet in three weeks time.

So three weeks passed, and the day of the meet arrived. Matt turned up at the pool, saw his dreaded competitor, and.....immediately broke out into a huge smile! For the first time, looking at his rival, all he could think of was a *rabbit!*

The thoughts of fear and dread had been replaced with fun and laughter. His subconscious mind had completely erased the fear, and replaced it with a symbol, which represented no form of danger whatsoever (as I assume rabbits don't swim particularly well!).

So as soon as Matt spotted his rival, he knew at that moment he would not lose to him again, because he simply *no longer felt any fear*. And this was exactly what happened, as Matt beat him twice that day, and did not lose to him for the following six months in the pool.

Mind Training for Swimmers

This technique has worked well for many swimmers since then, and each time it has erased the fear and the intimidation. Try this, you might be surprised at the results.

I had another National swimmer tell me how she used this method, and that she had all the entire blocks of the pool filled with an array of different animals! She said it was rather easy (I imagine she had a rather well-developed imagination) as there was one swimmer who had a rather long neck, who she pictured as a giraffe, another swimmer had curly blonde hair, so she instantly became a sheep, etc. The next swimmer she mentioned was "a cow" (I think purely because she didn't like this swimmer!).

Imagery For Coping With Pressure

This is a powerful method that has achieved some great results for swimmers who are feeling the glare of attention on them before a race (often because they are considered the favourite to win). If you feel that you would prefer to swim *without* the glare of attention upon you (and I only mention this as some swimmers actually perform better when the focus is *upon* them), then this is what you do.

Visualize the race about to begin, and as you mentally look at the pool from the starting block, imagine that your *lane is draped with black curtains along both sides of your lane.* These curtains prevent anyone being able to see your race, and so this allows you to swim as if no one was watching - letting you swim your own race, and also without worrying about the other lanes.

Mind Training for Swimmers

This is a fabulous method to use when the 'spotlight' is on you and you are feeling the pressure of being the favourite. A top Australian coach created this visualization for world-record breaking swimmer Susie O'Neill towards the end of her career, to help her deal with all the media attention she was getting as she endeavoured to break a long-standing world record (which she eventually did). Try it out and see if it helps take the pressure off you.

Imagery For Positivity / Energy

This is a great method that one of my clients created for herself a few years ago, and the technique works beautifully. It's very useful whenever you are feeling negative, low in confidence, or even low in energy, and believe it or not, you can even use this visualization whilst walking around in the normal awakened state, as well as visualizing it the normal way with eyes closed. This is a highly effective use of imagery, utilising the way your subconscious translates the colours of gold or yellow to represent *energy*. Here's what you do:

As you are walking along (or otherwise *visualizing* walking along), imagine a *beautiful vibrant golden waterfall* flowing down in front of you. You are going to walk right through this fabulous waterfall, and when you do, you will see it cleanse all the negativity or lethargy from your mind and body, leaving you feeling glowing with positivity and energy.

See the waterfall filling your body with this pure golden energy and positivity, cleansing every negative atom from your body. Then when you emerge on the other side of the waterfall, you will often feel cleansed, pure and fabulous, as if you really have just walked through a waterfall of positive energy.

Using Imagery: How a Swimmer Overcame Her Problems By Erasing a Swim From Her Past!

It may seem strange, but sometimes even your *past* can be a factor, which can hold you back from reaching your peak. A particularly bad swim from the past, or any traumatic event that occurred during swimming, can haunt a swimmer for a long period of time, and hold them back from reaching their true potential if the issues are not dealt with. Strangely enough, these issues can almost become like lead weights around a swimmer's legs if left unattended.

For instance, one swimmer I was working with was having some unusually slow progress whilst using my program, and so I thought I should delve a little deeper to try to find the problem. I asked her if she could remember any particularly terrible swims, or swimming events, from the past which she wished she could "go back in time" and change. And immediately, tears came to her eyes.

The story unfolded that some years before, she had swum a race for her school, which was having a swimming carnival against another rival school that was their prime competitor each year. At the end of the day the two schools were locked in a tie, and so they decided to run an I/M event to decide the winner, and this girl was to represent her entire school in this race, against one swimmer from the other school.

Mind Training for Swimmers

During the race she was leading most of the way, and her school friends and teachers were loudly screaming out their support, all of them assuming that their school was about to win as she was looking to be the likely winner. Unfortunately the other girl came through in the late stages and won the race by a few hundredths of a second – and this was a huge letdown, not only for her but also for her school.

For the next 3-4 years she felt that she had let her friends and the entire school down, but had kept this mental anguish to herself, bottled up inside. We later found that this had caused most of her problems in swimming, *all of which completely disappeared* when she began using a technique I am about to mention, which released that painful memory and allowed her to swim freely again. This technique virtually allows you to go back in time, and have a chance to swim that race over once more. This is how we did it:

First of all, I asked her to *relax and vividly imagine* that race each day, but with a major difference. Instead of seeing the race as it had actually happened, I asked her to completely *change the final result* of the race, every single time she visualized it, so that she would actually be able to go back and *win the race* each time, in her mind.

She struggled to do this initially, and the exercise even brought a quite a few tears at first, but she managed to do this exercise daily for a month or two, and sure enough, her swimming results began to improve. Her improvements were slow at first, taking small amounts off her PB's, and then they became far more dramatic, with major seconds being taken off her times. As it seemed that the problem had been

Mind Training for Swimmers

successfully cleared, we then finished with that exercise and changed her back to visualizing her upcoming events.

Interestingly, around six months later I asked her about that old school race again, and asked her what she felt about it. And guess what she said? She *could no longer even remember* what had happened in the race, or who had won it! Through some visualization work, the painful memory of that loss had been completely erased by her memory bank, and so it was no longer an issue for her. And more importantly, it no longer held her back in her current swimming meets.

This technique has since worked for many others, by releasing some of the past traumatic memories, and consequently freeing up this valuable energy to be used more positively in future races.

Take Yourself Through A 30 Second Visualization
Just Before The Race

When you are waiting for your race to be called, take 30 seconds to just look at the pool and mentally imagine yourself swimming the race of your life. Remind yourself that *the water is your friend,* and will be your partner in success to help you achieve your dreams – which is along the lines of something I believe the great swimmer Alex Popov once said.

Many swimmers can visualize this quite easily by just looking at the pool with their eyes open, simply imagining yourself already in the pool - or, if there is a race already going on (especially if there is a clear leader), imagine yourself *as being the leader.* Of course, you do this

Mind Training for Swimmers

without actually *watching* either the swimmer, or their stroking technique, in any great detail. The idea is obviously not to copy that swimmer but to simply use their position in the race (i.e., first place) as a way of mentally projecting yourself into your upcoming and successful race. Needless to say, if another swimmer takes first place, you become *that* swimmer instead!

This is an extra boost of mental power you can give yourself directly before a race, which can even be done just before you walk to the block. Needless to say, earlier in the day it is highly advisable to do proper 10-15 minute visualization session to get your mind thoroughly focused upon success in your races that day.   If this cannot be arranged, make sure you have been doing some regular daily visualizations during the weeks before the meet, for your mind and body to tap into once you are on the block.

Imagery When Leading a Race

This is a little trick you play on your mind *during* races to prevent the *fear of being passed* coming into your mind when you are in the lead, which some swimmers seem to suffer from. I've noticed that many early leaders in races tend to focus upon the swimmers *behind* them, and become filled with fear *trying to protect their lead* instead of using this mental energy to focus upon the task at hand. This is exactly what their competitors are hoping they will do!

Instead, the leader needs to be thinking about something more positive, such as making their lead ever greater, and moving even further

Mind Training for Swimmers

ahead. One way of doing this is to *mentally create a new leader*. All you do is mentally pretend to yourself that you're actually in *second* place, behind an imaginary swimmer, instead of leading.

This completely changes your way of thinking, and your approach to the race, because your goal is now to speed up and *catch* the leader, instead of worrying about protecting your lead from the swimmers behind you. This works incredibly well for many swimmers, and allows you to move further ahead of the swimmers behind you, without worrying or being overly concerned about them.

If you have difficulty imagining a new leader, simply pretend that the imaginary leader is already onto the next lap and out of your view. This method keeps your mind focused upon the goal (instead of the obstacles), which is something I will be discussing a lot more later on in this book.

When Someone Tries To Pass You

Many swimmers panic when they realize that a competitor is attempting to pass them. This is a method you can use right there in the pool for times such as these, however I recommend you practice it in training first before trying it in meets.

First of all, when you realize someone is trying to pass you, you imagine that your body is suddenly filled with energy (which you can visualize as *glowing light* if you wish). You imagine this energy surging throughout your body (and when you get really accomplished at this, you can actually *feel* this happening), and then this energy transfers into

Mind Training for Swimmers

your strokes, as you find yourself *going with*, or leaving behind, the competitor.

When you master this method, it becomes an automatic, subconscious mental trigger, so that your body responds in this way *automatically* as soon as you realize someone is trying to pass you. Eventually you may even stop worrying about these swimmers altogether.

Create Your Dream Race

This is a powerful method, as it uses all of your strongest memories of past swims to create a mental program for your body to follow.

What you do is go through your memory bank and remember all the best *individual segments* of a race you have ever achieved, from all the races you have ever swum in your life - and put them all together in the *one* race visualization.

For instance, you may remember the particular race where you did your best-ever dive, as well as the race where you swam your best-ever 50 metres, plus your best-ever turn, and your best-ever finish. You simply put these segments together in your mind and run your mind through them as if they were all performed in *one race* (instead of 4 or 5 races).

This is a powerful way of not only remembering your all-time best performances, but to also use them productively to program yourself for future swims. It becomes your benchmark for the perfect race, and gives you something tangible to try and achieve – and guess what, it's *not* something that is out of your reach. Why? Because you have already done it all before! Just in different races, that's all.

Speed Up The Healing Process

Your subconscious mind controls your body's very powerful immune system, which takes care of the healing process within your body, and so it can also be used to help *accelerate* the natural healing process that takes place when you are hurt, sick or injured. These methods are commonly used in the health industry around the world nowadays - I have taught this technique, amongst others, to critically ill patients in hospitals, to help enhance the strength of their body's natural immune system. Needless to say, this visualization is to be used only as for *supplementary* use, in combination with whatever medications you may be prescribed by your doctor, so that both your medication and your body can work together to ensure a quick recovery. Whilst some people believe these methods are getting a bit 'out there', they have become almost mainstream throughout the world these days.

Here are three techniques which can help you with this area if you feel you need it, which should be incorporated along with your daily swim visualization until you feel that you no longer need it (if you don't need this information however, move onto "Troubleshooting Common Problems").

Mind Training for Swimmers

Healing Injury Method 1 – The Body Scan

Scan through different areas of your body as if you were an internal camera, focusing on any areas that are painful and, using imagery, make corrections to the areas that need attention.

For example: If you had a sore throat, you would visualize it being red and painful, and then you may cover it with an ice-cold spray which freezes it and takes away the stinging sensation. Or if you had congestion in the lungs, you may choose to use a suction device to clean the area out, and finish by cleansing it totally with a river of disinfectant, washing away all germs.

Any imagery that you create for yourself, and which feels genuine and authentic, can work very well - as all you need to do is convince your subconscious mind that this scenario is real (so it can go to work on it for you).

Healing Injury Method 2 - Breath Visualization

Imagine looking down at your body from above, seeing your body floating in a pool, on your back (this shouldn't be difficult for you!). Imagine that you can see that your body is completely transparent, and you can actually see the *irritated* area within your body, because the irritation is showing up as the colour red.

Now begin to see the irritated redness slowly flowing *out* of your body, and into the pool, totally dissolving and disappearing in the water.

Mind Training for Swimmers

Feel this redness leaving your body and continue until all redness has been dissolved, and your body is clear and transparent all over.

Next, see those areas begin to glow with a *bright golden light* (as your subconscious mind interprets this colours as the colour of healing), bathing those irritated areas in warmth, health and healing. *Feel* the warmth in these areas of your body as you do this. This light spreads right through to the rest of your body until your entire body is glowing in the healing light, and you can *feel* your body pulsating in the warmth of this vibrant light you have created.

Then slowly imagine the light ebbing away, and leaving your body now completely clear and thoroughly cleansed, looking perfect once more. Follow this by now switching your visualization to a scene of yourself swimming easily and effortlessly *without* the ailment, completely fit, strong, and without pain.

Healing Injury Method 3 - Breath Visualization

Here is another method you can use to boost your immune system and accelerate your rate of healing. This method can also be done in an awakened state with eyes closed.

Take in a deep breath and imagine filling every inch of your lungs with pure, cleansing oxygen which rejuvenates your body, and which filters out to all your body's major organs. Then breathe out, and imagine all negative material leaving your body with the out breath, such as stress, congestion etc - which may have been preventing your body from being in perfect health. Repeat for up to 10 breaths.

Mind Training for Swimmers

OK, that is the list of imagery exercises you can incorporate into your visualization - which pretty much covers most situations. Experiment with whichever methods you feel you need and which work best for you.

Troubleshooting Common Visualization Problems

Some people have a lot of trouble visualizing, and others find it the most natural thing in the world. The main thing to remember is that, like anything, you get better the more you practice, so don't worry if at first you find it difficult. Here are few common problems people come across, and ways you can overcome them.

I Have Trouble Seeing Images In My Mind.

If you find you have trouble 'seeing' any pictures in your mind, don't worry about this - simply *feel* the swim instead, including all the emotions that you would normally feel after a fabulous swim. Using your feelings during visualization works absolutely fine and can be just as effective as seeing great images, if not more so. Seeing the images is simply icing on the cake, so don't worry about this too much.

Thoughts Keep Coming Into My Mind And Interrupting The Visualization.

This simply means your mind is not relaxed enough, so do some extra deep breaths as well as some extra counting down backwards, and stay in your sanctuary a little longer until you feel your mind has gone

Mind Training for Swimmers

somewhat *drowsy*. Relaxation music can also help with this. If the problem continues, consider using my visualization CD at www.swimpsychology.com

Should I Visualize Looking From Inside My Body, Or Looking At My Body From Up Above The Pool?

It doesn't matter, as either or both of these approaches are fine – you can use a little of each if you wish, or whichever suits you best.

I Keep Visualizing Losing The Race, Or Seeing Negative Things Happen.

Simply cross the negative image out, by putting a big black cross through it, and then replace the images with new positive ones. You are the director and star of the movie, so you can re-shoot any part of the movie that you don't like, to make sure that it suits you perfectly.

I Go To Sleep Whenever I Try To Visualize.

Try visualizing in a sitting position instead (which is recommended), as lying down will often send you to sleep when you close your eyes, which is an automatic program we have had set up since the time of birth. If you already are visualizing sitting down, make yourself a fraction more uncomfortable, so that you will remain awake. Eg. Put a cushion underneath one buttock before you begin your visualization.

Mind Training for Swimmers

I Can't 'See' My Own Body When I Visualize.

That's OK - try visualizing the images from the viewpoint of your own eyes as you swim (rather than looking at your body, from up above), or even imagine yourself as one of your own favourite champion swimmers if you wish, as this imagery surprisingly works just as well.

In Closing

The main thing with visualization is to DO it. It is one of the most transformational techniques we have available, so use it whenever you can, and *regularly,* if you really want to get results. Here is your summary for this chapter, containing one compulsory mental exercise for your Mental Training Program.

Summary Of Essentials For Successful Visualization

- Mental Training Program:
  Daily visualization for 10-15 minutes for 6 weeks (generally focused upon the next meet coming up). Schedule the time to do your visualization each day. Tick off the days you have done the exercise. Monitor your results, and after the 42 days you *may* reduce it to 8-12 minutes a day, but only if you wish to do this. Visualization is one of the most crucial parts of the program. The discipline to do this separates the

Mind Training for Swimmers

champions from the 'wannabes'.

Your visualization can be done in 3 different ways:

- Using your own home-made music CD or iPod, or
- Without any music, or
- Using the Mind Training for Swimmers CD, which can be found at my website.

An additional 5-10 minute visualization before races would also be highly recommended. Get into a relaxed state before visualizing, by taking some deep breaths and mentally counting backwards, slowly from 20 down to zero. Alternatively, for those *not* doing early-morning training, first thing in the morning upon awakening is the ideal time to visualize your races – as right after awakening you will not require any form of relaxation, so you can begin your race visualization immediately.

- Make the images of the meet in your mind *vivid* and *real* by using all your senses. ie. 'See' the people, the competitors and the pool (noticing all the associated colours that should appear in the picture), 'hear' the sounds of the races, the water and the voices, notice the smell of chlorine, and most importantly, *feel the joy of winning* when you win the race in your mind, or swim a great time.
- *Always* see yourself swim a great, positive race in your mind. Never, *ever* lose a race in your head!

Mind Training for Swimmers

- Try using some *imagery* in your daily visualization - such as the dolphin / torpedo method, or the light and energy method.

- Vary your visualizations, make them interesting and regularly change the pool and the swimmers to make it a fresh and new visualization experience.

- Music can work well for visualizing races each day. This can add a special emotional content to your visualizations, which makes the process more powerful and authentic.

- Use visualization to reverse intimidation and allow you to feel in control.

- Use the 'sanctuary' relaxation method to overcome nerves at the pool, but not for more than 10 minutes. Even just a few minutes in your sanctuary can take the edge off your nervousness.

CHAPTER 5

The Power Of Words

Let's move on to a new technique – affirmations (often known as mantras), which like visualization, can be used to pre-program your race, as well as improve consistency, belief, and create a more positive attitude.

Affirmations can be used for a quick boost directly before races, or whenever you're going through common problems such as feeling low in confidence or being nervous before a race. They can also be applied to long-term uses as well, just like visualization.

Affirmations are the process of mentally repeating a few words over and over again in your mind. This bombards your subconscious with *one positive thought*, again and again, until it eventually accepts the thought as a command and begins to act upon it.

For instance, let's say that you swam a heat and found you had a problem with your stroking rhythm, which meant you were losing your usual power and speed. Often this would mean that your conscious mind had been thinking *negative or erratic thoughts,* which were

Mind Training for Swimmers

processed through your system and caused erratic results in your performance.

This would be a great time to use an affirmation, before you swam in the next race. You would repeat a phrase to yourself, over and over again in your mind for about ten minutes - let's say something like "perfect rhythm, perfect rhythm, perfect rhythm".

This technique prevents your conscious mind from thinking destructive thoughts, whilst at the same time, it bombards your subconscious with a single positive thought - until finally your subconscious begins co-ordinating your "perfect rhythm".

You see, your subconscious controls all your movement and co-ordination, and so it's very important to give it the right commands!

Affirmations work very effectively for swimmers. It's a little like *talking to ourselves,* but don't worry, there is nothing strange about this - because believe it or not you've been talking to yourself *all your life!* Every person, either knowingly or unknowingly, mentally talks to himself or herself almost every moment they are awake – and so this also means that every swimmer talks to himself or to herself before a race!

There is a constant inner-dialogue going on in our head, virtually every minute of the day. The problem is, this inner talk is not always as positive as we'd like it to be, and often we have no idea just how negative our inner dialogue can be. Often before a race, our thoughts are about the various things that we are worried about, or which might possibly go wrong – instead of thinking how *good* we are, and of all the

Mind Training for Swimmers

things that could go right. After a bad race, many swimmers will mentally abuse themselves with thoughts such as "you idiot! You're so useless! You can swim better so much better than that, how could you be so stupid!", or something similarly scathing, and it's times like these that affirmations come in really handy.

Instead of worrying, thinking negatively, or mentally abusing yourself, instead repeat a positive affirmation to yourself, in your mind. By repeating it over and over again, an affirmation stops this constant flow of negative thoughts, and helps to program your subconscious positively for your next race – rather than showing up for your next event in mental tatters!

Directly after a bad race is an important time to use this technique, especially if you have more races that day - as it can prevent you from blowing the remainder of your races from a tirade of self-abuse. So many swimmers fall into this trap, so don't be one of them!

It's estimated that 60,000 thoughts a day are going through your mind – and as this is a vast number of thoughts, there is no real way we can possibly keep track of all of them. So by using the affirmation technique, you actually get to *choose* what you would like your mind to think, just for a few moments - instead of allowing it to run rampant as it usually does. It is the ultimate way to take control of your thoughts, even just for a short time.

All great athletes and swimmers have used affirmations at some time in their careers, whether they actually realised they were using them or not. Possibly the greatest boxer of all-time was Muhammad

Mind Training for Swimmers

Ali, who won the world heavyweight boxing title 4 times in his career. Strangely, rather than repeat the affirmation *silently* to himself as most people do, he said it out loud - to his opponents, the media, and anyone else that would listen! What was his mantra? "I am the greatest!"

Back in the 1970's, most people thought Ali was simply being egotistical - which quite probably, he was! However, what they *didn't* realise was that *not only* was he chanting this line to intimidate his opponent, but he was also programming his own subconscious with a powerful affirmation - that he was the greatest boxer of all time. Needless to say, this turned out to be true - he became the greatest boxer of his era, and possibly of all time.

The Australian Olympic gold medallist Susie O'Neill mentioned in her autobiography "Choose To Win" that she used the rather unusual affirmation "loose as a goose" before her races, because she found it humorous and it had the desired effect of relaxing her mind and body.

Most top swimmers and athletes use some form of affirmation before a big race, so let's have a closer look at how they work, and how use them properly.

How To Use Affirmations

Affirmations are the most simple and convenient technique we have available, because unlike visualization, you don't even need to be in a state of relaxation to do them - you can do them anytime at all! You might be waiting for a race, walking, travelling in the car, walking to or

Mind Training for Swimmers

from school, waiting for a bus, in a queue or line up…you can use them virtually anytime you are not *mentally occupied* with another task.

Just to confirm once and for all (and you will be really relieved to know this) is that affirmations do *not* need to be repeated aloud. You simply repeat them silently in your mind, which prevents you getting some rather strange looks from other people! So this opens up a whole range of opportunities as to when you might happen to use them – and the great part is that no one will have any idea what you are doing.

So all you do is mentally repeat the affirmation to yourself over and over again in your mind, for a minimum of thirty times in a row. It's that easy, and you can also target affirmations towards virtually *any area* of your performance that you may need – such as to increase your speed, rhythm, confidence or relaxation.

However, there are some important things to know about affirmations – because, just like visualization, if you use them negatively, they can have a truly *disastrous* effect on your swimming. And, again like visualization, lots of swimmers do this without even knowing it.

Short And Long Term Affirmations

First of all, there are affirmations for both short-term goals and also long-term goals. For instance, if you're feeling *chronically* nervous before a race, obviously you need to change this situation fairly quickly. Before I go any further, I should point out that there is *normal*

Mind Training for Swimmers

nervousness (which is good for performance) and *chronic* nervousness (which is not so good).

So you find you have chronic nervousness before a race. What you'd do is repeat an affirmation in your mind constantly, for 5-10 minutes before the race - something like "I'm calm and relaxed. I'm calm and relaxed. I'm calm and relaxed". Or if you needed a boost of power for your race, you might try something like "power and speed, power and speed, power and speed" - and slowly but surely, you'll become more relaxed or confident as time goes on.

The effect of repeating an affirmation for 5-10 minutes may last for a few hours - but certainly not for days, weeks or months. This is because it's a short-term affirmation, designed to help you *almost immediately.*

But for more permanent, long-term improvement, simply repeating an affirmation for five minutes won't help you - it would require regular use of an affirmation over weeks or months to make a major difference. This would mean using at affirmation at various intervals throughout the day, for 3-5 minutes at a time, over the course of a couple of weeks or even several months. Needless to say, you would also be using the visualization technique in conjunction with the affirmation, so you are programming yourself with two powerful techniques each day.

This is what I recommend to achieve your goals - the combined use of both affirmations and visualization, as these techniques form a very potent partnership, which can truly move mountains – and help you

Mind Training for Swimmers

achieve your goals much more quickly. This partnership can also be used to help overcome and *reverse* long-term problems such as low confidence, chronic or extreme nervousness, etc.

For long-standing problems such as these, you would need to use an affirmation 50 times or more, each and every day - until you feel you are getting the results you want. For instance, a person with low confidence might use a daily affirmation such as "I have unlimited potential", "I'm unbeatable" or "I'm getting better every day" - or they may even use different affirmations on different days. Incredibly simple, isn't it? And for overcoming long-term problems, they would continue using an affirmation (and visualization) until they felt that the problem had reduced substantially, or disappeared completely – before targeting the techniques onto other areas.

Affirmations help to *reinforce our positive aspects* such as confidence, belief, relaxation, speed or endurance (depending on what affirmation you choose to use). There are several tricks to make them work correctly, however – so here we go.

Making Affirmations Work

Here are some important tips to make sure that your affirmations work effectively. Firstly, when you repeat your affirmation you must use *tremendous repetition* – it must be repeated over and over, and over again. Otherwise the mantra simply gets lost in all the mental chatter constantly going on in your conscious mind. The only way to make this

Mind Training for Swimmers

technique work is to repeat the affirmation for a *minimum* of 2-3 minutes.

Of course, the more you repeat the affirmation, the better your chances of creating positive change more quickly, so there is no limit to how many times you wish to repeat an affirmation, and no risk of 'overdosing' on them.

For long-term goals, doing some daily affirmations just means taking the opportunity at any time whenever you don't need to *consciously* concentrate on something. Walking, waiting for a bus, during short breaks in your day - just take the opportunity whenever you can, and repeat an affirmation to yourself. The bonus is that no one knows that you are doing them – and you can easily stop anytime someone begins talking to you, and later recite some more, whenever the opportunity arises.

Of course, once you feel happy with the results you're getting, change your affirmation and focus on a different area of your performance you may wish to boost.

But the most powerful and dramatic time to use this technique is right before a race, for 5-10 minutes solid – which is a mandatory part of your Mental Training Program.

For these affirmations right before you compete, it's simply a matter of repeating them over and over in your mind for ten minutes - you might wish to do these affirmations before you are called for your race, or you might prefer to use them while you are in the marshalling area. As affirmations can also help you deal with nervousness in the

Mind Training for Swimmers

marshalling area, and block out negative thoughts which tend to attack us at this crucial time.

Of course, if someone asks you a question during this time, just temporarily stop reciting the affirmations and answer the person, but then go right back into reciting your affirmations again. After a few minutes of doing this, you may sometimes notice your subconscious has actually 'programmed it in', and you will sometimes hear your mind repeating the affirmation back to you, even whilst you're speaking to someone!

It's vital to keep your affirmations nice and short, so they're easy to repeat over and over again. This makes things much easier – I remember someone showed me an affirmation once that was half a page long! No way - this is much too long, always keep them short and easy to repeat.

The exact wording of affirmations is also pretty important. For instance, if you used an affirmation like "*I'm better than I was*", this would totally confuse your subconscious, because it wouldn't understand *when* you were talking about! And of course, the affirmation would have no affect whatsoever. A better affirmation in this case would be "I'm better than ever" – which also happens to be an easier affirmation to repeat.

Two other very important qualities that affirmations must possess is they must be *worded positively*, and also in the *present tense*. Basically this means never use *downbeat*-sounding affirmations, such as "I won't lose" - because that would be just *asking* for trouble! A word

Mind Training for Swimmers

such as 'lose' just *isn't* what you want your mind to be hearing right before a race, because there is a good chance it just might take you seriously!

When I mentioned that an affirmation must be worded in the *present tense,* I meant that it needs to be worded as if it is really happening *right in the here and now*, not at some time in the future. So even if you're training for a meet that is in a month's time, make sure your affirmation sounds as if it's actually *already* happening. For instance, "I always win finals" would then be a better affirmation than "I *will* win the final", because your mind will automatically ask "*when* do you want me to win the final?" In ten years? And so there would be no response from your mind, or body for that matter. So always create your affirmations in the present tense.

As I mentioned earlier, affirmations are the most convenient technique in the world, as you can use them virtually any time of the day, and no-one has any idea whatsoever that you are doing your mental training! It certainly makes queues or line-ups much easier, because going into your affirmations makes the time go much quicker – you may even get a little disappointed if the line-up moves too fast, and you don't have time to repeat more of them! You can even use this technique in your training or practice - reciting them over and over in your mind to the *exact rhythm* of your strokes! This is also especially easy for long-distance or open water swimmers.

A couple of good *speed* affirmations are "I swim like lightning" and "power and speed" – but there is always an exception! No one - no,

Mind Training for Swimmers

not even myself - can tell you *exactly* what affirmations to use, because only *you* truly know the specific words that will inspire and motivate you. No one else can do this for you - all I can do is *guide you* with examples, which you can peruse and decide whether you like them or not. This is the acid test - if you *like* the sound and the feeling of the affirmation, then it's probably a good one for you, and should create some results for you. Likewise, if you don't like the affirmation, don't use it, because it simply will not bring any results for you.

For instance, "I am the greatest!" might have worked fabulously well for Muhammad Ali, but it would not necessarily work for you. You must remember you are an individual who has different mental needs to others, and so these need to be custom-made to suit your own personality and mindset.

Apart from the list of affirmations I will provide for you, you can also try creating some of your own. When you do this, use words that give you a *buzz* and make you feel good when you say them – words that affect you on any emotional level. Your affirmations must be *inspiring*, and never boring such as the dreary mantra "I swim well" – which I doubt would motivate anyone! Instead, use words which make a real emotional *impression* upon you, such as "I'm swimming *brilliantly!*"

So once again, just to reinforce the point - use words that give you power and energy, that make you feel good by just *saying* them. That is what makes a powerful affirmation.

Mind Training for Swimmers

Here are some popular examples of affirmations, just to give you an idea, which can be used both before races and also on a daily basis. You will find you will like some of these and dislike others, or you may prefer to create some others of your own. The affirmations you *like* will be the most effective for you.

Grab a pen now, and jot down any affirmations that you like from this list, because you are going to make a *personal list* of affirmations for your future use. Here is the list:

Examples Of Affirmations

Lightning speed	Perfect swim
Power and speed	Steady and consistent
Everything is flowing perfectly	Perfect rhythm
Focused and confident	I'm unstoppable
I'm fit, fast and confident	I'm fast and strong
Power and courage	I can handle anything
Everything is going perfectly	Nothing can stop me
No-one can stop me	I have unlimited potential
I'm the best	I swim like lightning
Easy and effortless	Power swim
Lightning swim	I have unlimited potential
I'm a quick starter	I always finish strongly
I'm better than ever	I have unlimited energy
I'm in peak condition	I'm unbeatable
I'm a torpedo in the water	I feel great

Mind Training for Swimmers

I'm constantly improving	Perfection
My rhythm is perfect	I always win finals
I have unlimited potential	Calm and relaxed
I'm getting (better / faster) every day	Tranquil and serene
Everything is flowing perfectly	Easy and relaxed
I'm faster and stronger than ever	Peace and harmony
I'm fit, strong and powerful	Carefree and calm
Peace flows through me	I am phenomenal
I swim faster and stronger every day	I win easily and effortlessly

I'm getting (better / faster / stronger / more confident) every day

These Are The 8 Most Popular Affirmations (I've Encountered) For Before Races:

- Power and Speed
- Perfect Rhythm
- I Feel Great
- I have Unlimited Energy
- I'm Unbeatable
- I'm Calm and Relaxed
- I'm Better Than Ever
- Nothing Can Stop Me

Remember that these are all purely examples, as you might come up with some better ones of your own. Look through the personal list you have (hopefully!) created, and think which affirmation would be

Mind Training for Swimmers

best to begin with for your regular *daily* use. It should be focused towards a long-term goal you'd like to achieve, or a long-term problem you would like to overcome. Put a ring around one that fits this description, and write 'daily' next to it.

Now, scan your list and decide on an affirmation that you can use *directly before a race* at your next meet. Underline this one, and write 'pre-race' or *'before races'* next to it.

Do not lose this list, as these affirmations you have chosen will be used in the your mental training program - and those two you have chosen will be the first affirmations you will use. You will probably want to regularly change your affirmations however, as otherwise they can become overly familiar and stale, and so using some new ones makes the technique fresh and powerful again.

I recommend you put the list of these affirmations in a special exercise book I will discuss later in the 'lists' chapter. You can add to (or subtract from) this list of affirmations anytime, and the affirmations you use *can be changed at any time* if you feel they are not right for you. Tailor them to suit your needs at the time, that is the fabulous thing about this technique - its total flexibility and convenience.

Affirmations can also be used to overcome those particular times when you find that you are feeling a little negative or down, as they interrupt the negative flow of thoughts going on in your mind, and insert new, fresh positive thoughts. So keep this technique in mind for those times when you are not feeling overly positive, and need to break out of

Mind Training for Swimmers

the mental rut with a boost of positive energy. I will discuss more about this later in the next chapter.

Like visualization, some swimmers find this technique a little *different* or even *weird* to begin with, because they've often never encountered it before. This is what I tell those people: First of all, I ask them if they consider the champion swimmers to be a *little different to the others*, or just like everyone else - and their answer is almost always "of course they're different to the others!" Then I mention that if the champions *are* different to the other swimmers, then they must *do* something different as well - otherwise they wouldn't be different!

So the choice becomes: you can either do what everyone else *does* and be like everyone else, or you can do something a little different - like the champions, and be a little different to everyone else. Let's face it, who wants to be just another face in the crowd anyway?!

If you're *really* serious about creating a mental training program for yourself, and not giving up in the first month (which the average swimmers do) mark down the days that you have done your mental exercises. Once you've done these exercises for 6-8 weeks, you will find that you will be in a strong routine, and it will be easy from then onwards. The hard part is to keep it up for the first six weeks; and it's during *this time period* that those who succeed are separated from those who don't.

Affirmations and visualization are powerful ingredients that work very well together, and can be used to overcome almost any problem that you may encounter – in or out of the pool. Human beings

Mind Training for Swimmers

use their minds to think in 3 very different ways - in *pictures, feelings and words* (or for those who like the technical lingo – visual, kinaesthetic, and auditory). By using both the techniques of visualization and affirmations, it means that you are programming your mind for success using a very potent combination of *all three methods* – as visualization uses pictures and feelings, and affirmations utilizes words.

You can focus these techniques on any particular area in the same way a magnifying glass focuses the power of the sun, and you can create major improvement in a relatively short time. It doesn't matter whether you need to gain more confidence, swim faster, have greater endurance, increase your energy, motivation, determination, overcome technical weaknesses or swimming pain, or even assist the healing of injuries faster, it can all be done using the enormous power of your mind.

When you've created a daily routine using these techniques, they form a powerful, automatic boost to your performance and confidence, and you will feel more in control and at peace when you are getting ready to compete. When done regularly, they can help you to smash through the barriers that have been holding you back for years, and unleash your true potential to the world. So be disciplined, and patient, and you will meet with success that even *you* didn't know was possible.

Essentials For 'Talking To Yourself' Effectively

- Repeat a positive affirmation *constantly* for 5-10 minutes, just before races.

- Repeat a positive affirmation whenever you have nothing to think about in particular - eg. walking, waiting for a bus/train, in a queue or line-up, etc.

- Keep the affirmation short and easy to repeat.

- Keep it positive, with no negative words

- Word the affirmation as if it is already happening right here in the present time, not as if you are waiting for it to happen some time in the future.

   eg. "I swim like lightning" <u>NOT</u> "I *will* swim like lightning".

Affirmations are best used:

- Before races

- Whenever you are feeling nervous

- Whenever you feel down or negative

- For at least a few minutes each and every day

How Many Affirmations Can You Use?

I am often asked if a swimmer can use more than one affirmation. The answer is yes, you can use two or sometimes three at a time if you wish. The main thing is to use just one at a time, reciting it at least fifty times before you consider going onto another.

Mind Training for Swimmers

It's also important to use the affirmation that is right for you at the time - you might use a particular affirmation before one race, but a completely different one before your *next* race, if that happens to feel right for you. I would definitely limit it to three however, so your mind does not get too jumbled up - you want it to be able to focus on only one or two main areas at a time, rather than spreading its focus too thinly.

For daily affirmations it's also possible to use more than one affirmation - you can even use a particular one in the morning, another around lunchtime and yet another to finish the day, if you wished. Generally I recommend one affirmation at a time however, so that you can achieve quicker results in the area you choose to focus upon, before moving onto other areas.

Now we must move onto another subject essential for your future success - creating a positive thought pattern. This is an aspect that unfortunately has the power to override and negate all the powerful techniques I have shown you (if we are not careful), but it also has the power to make these techniques even stronger. Here is your summary for this chapter, containing one compulsory exercise for your Mental Training Program, plus another suggested exercise.

Summary

- <u>Mental Training Program:</u>
  Repeat your 'pre-race' affirmation for 5-10 minutes silently to yourself before all races.

Mind Training for Swimmers

- <u>Mental Training Program:</u>

  Repeat your daily affirmation for 3 minutes each day. This can create long-term change.

CHAPTER 6

An Essential Quality For All Successful Swimmers

Something all champions possess is the ability to remain positive and overcome their own doubts and negative thoughts. It's one of the toughest things to do for a swimmer, because negative thoughts are the stumbling block that every competitor must overcome before they truly become a champion.

This is an essential part of your mental training - because this is the *one* aspect, if not monitored closely, which can de-rail your dreams by preventing your visualization and affirmation techniques from working effectively.

Basically a swimmer who thinks negatively most of the time and expects the worst can forget making the big-time, as it wouldn't matter how much they visualized or affirmed. Only a *positive* attitude will allow these techniques to work as they are meant to.

This is not to say that great swimmers don't have negative thoughts, quite the opposite – but they control these thoughts and channel them into positive energy for their performance. They get their

Mind Training for Swimmers

minds focusing back onto the positive as soon as possible – because if they didn't, they simply would not have a swim career!

Don't worry, if you have some doubts about how you will go at an important meet, this is completely natural. However, you then have two options; you can ignore those worries and remain focused on how you *intend* to perform at the meet. Or, possibly you may begin to dwell on those doubts, which makes these your prime focus instead of performing well at the meet. Focusing upon negative thoughts creates all kinds of mental monsters, which fill you with nerves and fear by the time the meet is about to begin. Your mind must always be focused positively to perform at your best every time - and until this becomes automatic, it will be a conscious choice you will have to make before each and every race, at each and every meet.

Why Positive Thinking Is Essential For Success

Maintaining a positive thought pattern is essential for two reasons. Firstly, it helps you maintain a *positive expectancy* before races (and swimmers tend to get what they expect, not what they deserve) plus it also helps to prevent any negative *beliefs* being created in your mind, which can have long-term effects down the track.

Any thought that you think *over and over again,* such as a negative thought such as "I can't beat John / Sarah" eventually creates a belief within your subconscious mind, and we have already discussed just how powerful these beliefs are in swimming.

Mind Training for Swimmers

Negative beliefs create recurring patterns in your performance that can be very hard to break. This is probably the most important *long-term* reason to remain positive mentally. Symptoms of negative beliefs may include major challenges such as being stuck on a particular 'personal best time' for many months or years (which often seems impossible to better), coming second to a particular competitor over and over again, swimming badly at a particular pool every time, making the same mistakes repetitively, etc – basically anything such as this which happens to you on a regular *recurring* basis.

So keeping our mind positive is essential to ensure that our beliefs remain positive as well. And, as you are about to read, it's not just your *own* negative thoughts you have to keep an eye on!

Don't Allow Yourself To React To Negative Thoughts

Unfortunately keeping our mind free of negative thoughts is not just a matter of watching over our own thoughts – we also need to keep a lookout for negative thoughts aimed at us from other people as well, which can be even more difficult to deal with. Once you become confident at handling negative comments from other people as well as your own self-doubts, it becomes a huge advantage whenever you're about to swim a race.

It's quite an important aspect to know that it's not actually negative people, or even negative thoughts, that affect you. It's your own *reaction* to those people, or those negative thoughts, which is the most important. There is no law that says you *have* to believe a negative

Mind Training for Swimmers

comment from someone, or that you must pay any attention to a negative thought.

The key is that it's always your *choice* as to how you react to these comments from competitors or other people - you are not a victim of a negative comment until you actually *choose to react negatively to it.* And if you refuse to emotionally react to negative comments, then you are simply not a victim of them – just a mildly interested observer who pays little notice to them.

For instance, let's say someone says to you before a race "there's no way you're going to beat that swimmer in the lane next to you". This means that you then have two choices - one is to dwell on this comment, which fuels it and allows it to become a mental monster. Otherwise you could choose to totally disregard it, and say to yourself, "How would *they* know what I can do?" (And even if they *do* know you reasonably well, it makes no difference – as it does not allow that you might dig deep and bring out something very special for that particular race).

You must choose to both completely ignore the negatives and *focus on the positives*, or you can choose to worry about all the things that could go wrong and allow them to turn you into an emotional wreck. It's your choice! And it seems like a very obvious choice too, yet it's amazing at just how many swimmers choose to listen to these 'voices of doom' and allow themselves to be sucked down into their negative energy.

The wonderful thing is that YOU have the power, every second of the day, to choose exactly what you would like to think! It's amazing

Mind Training for Swimmers

how few people realize this. From now on, choose to focus on the positive aspects *only*, and disregard negative comments from people - who eventually will know better than to bother wasting their time trying to upset you. I will delve into some techniques shortly that can help you with this.

Become Known As The Machine!

Once you manage to create a positive mindset that virtually never gets upset (or shows any *evidence* of being upset), eventually you will develop a reputation amongst other swimmers that absolutely nothing *ever* bothers you – and eventually those who know you will not even bother to try. When this happens, they virtually begin to start thinking of you as some type of swimming *machine*, who's totally unaffected by setbacks or doubts (a bit like the Terminator in the old Arnold Schwartzenegger movies!) and this is a big psychological advantage in your favour.

When they stop bothering to try and unsettle you before important races, it often means they have already become quite *psyched out* swimming against you. And why not? Let's face it, who wants to swim against a machine?

Throw Out The Uncontrollables

Worrying about *uncontrollables* is probably the greatest enemy of a swimmer before races. *Uncontrollables* are all the things that we simply have no control over whatsoever at a swim meet - such as how our competitors will perform, the amount of swimmers in the warm-up

Mind Training for Swimmers

pool, worrying if your goggles will fill with water, etc. Basically it is worrying about anything that *might go wrong.*

Uncontrollables are simply a total waste of valuable energy, as they are completely outside of your 'sphere of control' (i.e., things that you have some control over), and so it's imperative to constantly watch out for these 'saboteurs' before races. It is far more productive to focus upon the things you *can* control.

Once discovered, uncontrollables must be trashed immediately before they have time to affect upon your performance. This means that you need to ignore them, delete them, and forget them – whatever you have to do to ensure they have no power over you. Watch closely for these thoughts at every meet, as they can creep up on you when you least expect them.

The best methods for treating them are to either *cancel* them out completely (using the Delete Method I will show you shortly), or focus upon something else more positive, or even better, *reverse* the thought to its exact opposite - such as focusing upon how *well* everything is going to go.

When you have managed to stop yourself worrying about *uncontrollables*, it's amazing at how much extra energy it can inject into your swim – because worrying demands a lot of energy, believe me! So forget worrying altogether, just focus on how well the race is going to go. This will give you an advantage over 90% of your competitors, because whether you know it or not, THEY are all worrying about

Mind Training for Swimmers

uncontrollables themselves! So get the edge on the others and don't fall into this trap any more.

"What's Great About This?"

One fabulous way to deal with uncontrollables is to totally reverse your thought pattern by choosing to focus upon all the *great* things about the meet that day. To do this, you simply ask yourself a question - *"what's great about this?"*. And then you allow your mind to come up with the answers - and soon you have a whole bunch of them. For instance, you may come up with thoughts such as:

- I really like this pool
- My whole team are here supporting me
- This is my favourite event
- I am swimming pretty well at the moment
- Etc., etc.

The more answers you come up with, the more positive you will begin to feel, which will reverse the negative feelings that uncontrollables can bring. It's really easy to do this and it doesn't take long to find a whole host of positive reasons why you are actually in a *great* situation today – it's purely just a matter of forcing your mind to *ask the question,* and come up with the answers. I would highly recommend you ask yourself this question before every single race, at every single meet. It is a sure way of creating a positive mindset before you are on the block.

Mind Training for Swimmers

I read recently about a swimmer at the 2005 World Championships who won her event from the 8th lane - and said that she saw the lane as being a positive, not a negative. She reminded herself that being in this lane meant that no-one would be watching her closely, and so she had less pressure of expectation upon her than the other swimmers who were in the centre lanes. She turned this 'negative' into a positive, and became a world champion. It's all in *how you look at it.*

Use Tunnel Vision To Defeat The Uncontrollables

Tunnel vision is another way to deal with negative thoughts. Tunnel vision means focusing 100% on your goal, and 0% on the *obstacles in your way*. This also improves your concentration and focus and, as it helps to prevent negative thoughts, it gives you access to additional energy for your races, which you are no longer wasting on worrying.

When you are getting ready for a race, this is when the negative thoughts and doubts are most likely to appear, and try to break down your confidence – so keep an eye out for them. When you find yourself beginning to worry needlessly about all kinds of 'negatives', think of tunnel vision. Tunnel vision means focusing upon your goal *so completely* that you simply cannot see any obstacles getting in your way.

It is the exact *opposite* of worrying about uncontrollables - and a great way to deal with them (though don't forget the "what's great about this?" method as well).

Mind Training for Swimmers

Try this exercise for a moment: Imagine you are looking through a narrow tunnel, directly at your goal (just for realism, make a 'tunnel' with your hand and look through it with one eye at something on the other side of the room). You'll notice that the 'goal' (i.e., the object on the wall) is all you can see, as the tunnel prevents you from seeing anything else.

This is how tunnel vision works. Your goal – such as winning your race, or doing a good time - becomes *the only thing you can focus upon,* as there are absolutely no distractions or uncontrollables to worry about, because tunnel vision does not allow you focus upon anything but your goal.

Now, imagine that this tunnel is becoming wider and wider (open your hand out more and more until the whole room is in view), and suddenly you will see there are lots more 'distractions' going on, to prevent you focusing on your goal. These are the obstacles that get in your way before races (such as your other competitors), and they are the worst things you could possibly be focusing upon!

It's much better to simply focus upon your goal, than to try and focus on *everything all at once.* This is tunnel vision.

This is not to say that you shouldn't *be aware* of the obstacles - it's good to know what your competition is going to be like. However it's important not to focus or dwell upon them, as anything your mind focuses upon, expands. This means that if you worry about a particular competitor too much, your mind will eventually turn them into a *mental monster* and they will block your path to success.

Mind Training for Swimmers

So the choice is obvious - if you use *tunnel vision* you simply won't see the distractions or uncontrollables anymore, they will often disappear completely and you will not have to worry about them. Always remember that 99% of the things we worry about, never actually happen anyway.

Be On The Alert For Negatives At These Times!

Of course, there *are* particular times when it's definitely easier to be negative than positive, and these are the times you have to watch out for, most of all. Here are a few of the classic times to watch out for negative thoughts and self-abuse:

- Immediately after a not-so-great race - this is a classic time to mentally beat yourself up!
- Just before a big race – nerves can be jangling and it can be easy to think negatively
- When you are about to swim against someone you have never beaten
- When someone has made a nasty comment to you, about yourself or your swimming

These are the danger times when it's *easy* to think negatively, and the reason why these particular situations are worse than all the rest is because they're fuelled with powerful *emotion*.

When you mix a negative thought with powerful emotion, it becomes a major problem. It can have a major affect on your outlook for

Mind Training for Swimmers

the rest of the day, or sometimes even for weeks or months in extreme cases - and this can be fatal to a top swimmer. Emotions are great, but only when they're positive, uplifting ones. Otherwise they can be like a hammer, pushing you further downwards (and I'm not talking about your times). So in these particular situations you must make an Olympic effort to remain positive, and you can know that there is nothing surer than the fact that at the same time, your competitors will *also* be battling with their own negativity.

As I mentioned earlier, if you can demonstrate to onlookers that these situations *no longer bother you and will not stop you,* this can eventually set up a belief in your competitors' minds that you are a powerful swimming machine, who is simply unaffected by stressful situations. You simply can't put a *value* on something that good! So work on creating this impression in the minds of your competitors.

The Swimmer's Biggest Problem Directly Before Races

Directly before a race is the most crucial time mentally. During this time, probably the toughest obstacle a swimmer faces is *doubt in their own ability,* brought on by negative thoughts. These thoughts create fear in the mind of the swimmer, which can often be fatal to their chances and, as mentioned earlier, can bring on many other associated problems such as:

- Unusual or silly mistakes during the race
- Extreme nervousness (that sometimes even manifests as vomiting)

Mind Training for Swimmers

- Worrying about *uncontrollables*
- A deep inner feeling of *not being good enough*
- Intimidation from other competitors
- Negative thoughts of all types
- Low energy y
- Not looking forward to meets/races
- Jealousy of other swimmers

Visualization and affirmations can help to overcome all of these symptoms, as well as having a positive thought pattern - which of course is essential for these techniques to work properly. This positive mindset extends to the very conversations you have with other people as well – so make sure you don't say anything negative about your races before you go out to swim. Your subconscious is always listening, and just might take you seriously.

Train With Power

All these principles also apply to your daily practice, as this will condition your mind and body into being positive and strong at the meets. After each training session, think back to what you did *best* during those sets that day, and run the images of that stroke, lap or set all over again in your mind. This will build up a positive outlook to your training, which every swimmer knows is essential for long-term success.

Also, never dwell for too long upon the *difficulty* of training, such as the cold, the pain etc - just focus your mind instantly onto your

Mind Training for Swimmers

goal, and the reasons *why* you are training. Always keep your mind firmly on your goal, not the obstacles. Condition yourself to be *positive in all circumstances,* and then it will eventually become easy when you are at the meets! In fact, the goal is to become positive - not just in training or the meets, but ALL the time.

A top Australian Olympian once gave some revealing insights into the extent of his mental strength in an interview. The interviewer noticed he used the word "enjoy" a total of 78 times during the interview - and when questioned about this, he said that he deliberately used the word because swimming training was often hard work and that using the word "enjoy" *changed this way of thinking* about his training in his mind.

If your mind is focused upon the *negatives* of swimming practice or training, such as the pain, the early mornings, the social sacrifices etc - then all these negative things simply *increase in intensity* and just make it too hard to continue over a long period of time. So do your best to enjoy what you are doing, it's *vital* to success.

Your Mental Diet

Both the thoughts you think and the words you choose are either boosting you up, or creating roadblocks to your success. They do this by creating powerful beliefs or *programs* in your mind, which have a huge affect on your results.

Let me explain further. The *dominant* thoughts and the words that you continually use every day eventually become stored in your

Mind Training for Swimmers

subconscious where they create networks of new beliefs - and you already know how powerful beliefs are. Of course, this is fabulous news for those who *never* have a negative thought, but not so great for us mere mortals – so it's something we have to be on the lookout for all the time.

The amazing thing is that when I mention this to swimmers, 99% of them will tell me that they virtually never say, or think, anything negative - and that they have nothing to worry about in this regard. It's fabulous that their self-image can seem so strong, however in most cases I find it to be more often a case of being in complete *denial*. Often after informing me of how positive they are, they utter a negative statement within 30-60 seconds *without even realising it!*

This is exactly what normally happens. As many of our words and thoughts become so ingrained and *automatic* - because we've been saying or thinking them for so long - most of the time we don't even realize that we're often thinking negative thoughts, often for *many years* without even knowing it.

An example of a negative statement creeping into our everyday speech pattern might be something like, "Oh, you just can't win; can you?" Or another one is, "Absolutely no way!" These, if repeated often enough, create inner beliefs, which signal to your subconscious that there is absolutely *no way* that you deserve to win! Such was the case of the swimmer I mentioned earlier, who came in second place for the best part of 4 years.

Mind Training for Swimmers

Most people have no idea that they even *use* these expressions, let alone the *impact* they can have on their performance, and you often hear swimmers making negative statements before races – not thinking that their words might have any bearing upon their race.

Let me spell it out clearly - these thoughts and statements may only seem very minor and small, and they are - but multiply them by *thousands of repetitions* over the course of 6-12 months, and they can gain a great deal of power over you!

So it's necessary to begin watching and *policing* the thoughts that you are both *saying and thinking*, because they're going to have a major influence on where your swimming career is going. You literally have to eavesdrop on your own thoughts. This is not always easy, because I've already pointed out that many of the most destructive thoughts are *those that you do not even realise that you're thinking!*

It takes some powerful methods to *cleanse your thought pattern* of negative thoughts and doubts, in order to create a positive mindset. I call the process of this a Mental Diet, which is what most people need to do for a minimum of one month in order to begin noticing those *automatic, subconscious* negative thoughts, not to mention the negative words you may routinely use in your vocabulary without knowing. This will be part of your mental training program - going on the mental diet for a minimum period of one month, and weeding out those thoughts that may be holding you back.

The requirements of your one-month mental diet include, in this order:

Mind Training for Swimmers

a) Regularly "checking in" and eavesdropping on your own thoughts – and scanning for negatives

b) *Spotting* negative thoughts or words whenever they occur in either your thoughts or your conversations with people (and this step is the generally the hardest part of the whole process), before:

c) Mentally *erasing* the negative thought within your mind

d) Mentally *replacing* the thought with an opposite, positive thought, and finally:

e) *Continuing* to watch for more negatives to erase

Here are some effective techniques for dealing with negative thoughts of all kinds, which you can use to *erase and replace* negatives in your mental diet.

The Delete Method
(Used To Deal With Your Own Negative Thoughts)

Before I begin, I should mention that you should not be fooled by how simple this method appears to be - the fact is, the most effective techniques *are* the simplest ones, and this one really works! This method uses the mind just the way you would use a computer – which of course, in many ways it is.

For example, if I make a mistake whilst typing on my computer (which I did a minute ago), I simply erase it by highlighting the error

Mind Training for Swimmers

and then hitting the 'delete' button, before replacing it with the correct word - and this mental technique is virtually exactly the same process.

Now, would it be possible for me to *highlight, correct and replace* that particular error if I did not first of all *know it was there?* Of course not! And it's exactly the same with your mind - you can't correct negative thoughts if you don't know they are there - you have to spot them first. To do this, you need to begin *scanning and monitoring* both your thoughts and statements, daily. It's OK - not every single minute of the day – but just by simply doing a quick 'scan' of your thoughts ands statements every thirty minutes or so.

Doing this will divulge an amazing number of negatives that you did not even know *existed* in your thoughts – and, as I will mention in a moment, it will open up a whole new world to you that you did not even realise was there.

So the goal of this Mental Diet is to begin cleansing your mind of the thousands of *unconscious* negative thoughts and phrases which have become absolutely *automatic* in your everyday life, which may have been clogging your path to true success. And what a difference it will make!

The trick is to catch the negative thought while it's actually occurring at that very moment, because otherwise you simply will not spot it. But the good news is that, even though *at first* you may have to constantly remind yourself to consciously "scan your thoughts" every 30 minutes or so, this task will very quickly become automatic as well – until you find that eventually your mind will be doing almost constant

Mind Training for Swimmers

'automatic scans'. This means you will notice an incredible amount of negatives that you would normally never have even knew existed.

After you spot a negative thought, here is how you will mentally deal with it (followed by an example):

First of all, after noticing the negative thought, you immediately *cut the thought off* mid-sentence. You will then *erase* it, using a special *mental trigger* I will show you, and then last of all, you replace the negative thought with its *opposite*, a new thought that is far more positive. Here's an example, to make this process much clearer.

Let's say you're talking to a person who is asking you questions about your swimming, and how you think you might perform in a competition on the weekend. While you are answering them, you may suddenly notice that you are about to say something rather negative - eg. "I don't know how I'll swim on Saturday, I haven't been training very…" and then CUT! You instantly stop what you are about to say, and then (mentally) say to yourself "*Cancel that*, I'm going to swim brilliantly on Saturday."

You then change what you were *about* to say to the person, to a comment that is a little more positive, though it does not necessarily have to be overly-upbeat – it's more what you say to yourself *in your mind* that is the most important.

That is basically all there is to it - it's that easy, and it works very, very effectively. Simply stop the negative, erase it, and replace it with the positive. It's simple, but effective. The only catch is, you have to do this to *every time* you notice a negative thought - which means for

Mind Training for Swimmers

the first couple of weeks or even a month, you might be doing this quite a lot every day.

In fact, when you first embark on this mental diet, you will suddenly become aware of hundreds of negative thoughts - of your own, and also from other people - which you had never, ever noticed before. This can be a real eye opener! Negative comments you have never noticed before may even come from your family and friends - but remember, do not bother to try and change *them*, simply change the way you react to the negative thought (and make sure you do not accept it as being true).

I've always found it funny when I first teach this method to a young swimmer, and then they immediately begin using it - usually to point out every single negative word or statement their mother or father says during the next half hour! Whilst this is rather amusing, it is not really the goal of this method – though occasionally it can be helpful to make others more aware of creating a positive environment for you.

If you go and take a look at today's daily newspaper, and put a circle around every negative story, you will find 8 out of 10 will be negative stories. Negatives are virtually everywhere, and so it's important to filter out the 'garbage' so that your mind remains focused upon the positive. This is what will bring you your best results in the pool.

If you can remain on this mental diet for a month, continually throwing out the mental *garbage*, eventually your conscious mind will

Mind Training for Swimmers

reduce the amount of negatives it throws at you - and your times will prosper.

After a month on the Mental Diet, there will continue to be negative thoughts which will arise from your conscious mind, however your subconscious will then be *conditioned* to spot them immediately, and you can then easily cancel and replace them. Slowly but surely over time you can reduce your negative thoughts down to almost zero.

The Delete Method
(For Protecting Yourself From *Other* People's Negativity)

Here is another situation where you can use the Delete Method - when *someone else* has tried to put a negative thought in your mind (and you may be surprised to find that even the most well-meaning people can do this to test your mental strength).

For instance, you might be chatting to someone at the pool and they might say to you "So, I guess you don't expect too much from yourself this weekend, seeing that your times have been off lately?"

And suddenly you find that this comment has started you thinking, "Gee, maybe they're right, I *haven't* been swimming that well..." This is the crucial moment, where you will either accept that negative thought, or erase it forever.

This is the time to send that thought to the trash, using the Delete Method. Mentally say to yourself, "Cancel that, I'm going to swim a personal best time this weekend," and you will have nullified that

Mind Training for Swimmers

negative thought, and inserted a positive instead. It's easy to do and amazingly effective.

It really is like hitting the 'delete' button on your computer keyboard to erase mistakes - because your subconscious eventually recognizes that each time you use the word 'cancel'. It's a direct command to delete that statement from your memory bank. Remember, your subconscious takes commands from your conscious mind, so it has *no choice* but to erase that thought. Just as your computer cannot argue with you pressing the delete button, your subconscious does not argue with your conscious mind. It works just like a computer - in fact, when computers were originally invented, they were actually modelled directly ON the subconscious mind and its ability to store data!

So, just as you would with any computer, simply delete the mistake, and replace it with the new, positive data instead. If you continue to use this method, eventually you will have totally cleaned up your own mental "hard drive".

Continue to use this method *in your mental diet* every day for at least a month, until you find you have *much fewer* negative thoughts to cancel out. Soon you will be *thinking like a champion*, and your results will show the difference.

The Detachment Method

This method is quite different to the Delete Method, but it's also highly effective in dealing with negative thoughts. Let's say that you've just swum an important race, and that you *weren't* too impressed with

Mind Training for Swimmers

your swim. In fact, you're pretty *un*impressed! Often when this happens, swimmers get out of the pool and immediately begin mentally abusing themselves for not being good enough, being useless (etc, etc), getting emotional and some even having to hold back tears.

This is just *one way* of reacting to a bad performance. Not a great choice, and basically, *this approach creates an emotional wreck* that will, most probably, cause the swimmer to swim very badly in the next race, two hours later. A better approach would be having a good chat with yourself, something like this, "Okay, so that wasn't what I wanted. But that's history now. I can't change the result. In fact, I don't even care about that swim anymore. It's history. Gone. Erased. Forgotten. I'm not even going to give it another thought. I might think about how I can *improve* upon it, but I'm *not* interested in getting emotional about it, and I don't want to talk about it with anyone right now, unless it's in a positive way. I've got to focus on the positive, on my next race, instead of dwelling on that result. So what's my next race? Ah yes, my heat in 2 hours time - I'd better begin focusing positively on that one. Right now I'm going to get away from this atmosphere for a while, go and get some fresh air, relax a little, chat to some friends, and then begin to focus on the next race."

This method allows you to overcome the negative thoughts by simply *not getting involved in them*. Remember that the most dangerous negative thoughts are the ones that are fuelled with <u>emotion</u>, such as when you've just swum a particularly bad heat.

Mind Training for Swimmers

In essence, you are simply getting out of the pool and virtually saying to yourself "this is a classic time when I would normally be pretty upset with myself, but I *refuse to get involved* in this way of thinking!"

Now, even by reasoning with yourself, you may still feel some negative thoughts or emotion coming through, so what you do is *observe the thoughts,* not be involved *in* them. You simply watch them and say to yourself "it's only a negative thought, it can't affect me if I refuse to get involved in it". And so you become the *observer* of the thought, instead of the *thinker* of the thought.

This takes away the vital fuel the *negative* needs to survive because, without attention, the thought will simply wither and die. I call this the Detachment Method.

An additional way to ensure that these negatives are completely erased after using either this method or the Delete Method is to demolish them by reciting 20 or 30 positive affirmations. Just repeat a few short, positive statements to yourself over and over again, such as 'I'm a great swimmer'. This is a great idea after particularly *bad* negative thoughts that have threatened to affect your composure.

If you find that after particularly bad races that you tend to get emotional when you talk to people afterwards (and that you tend to snap at any well-meaning comments offered by friends or relatives!) then it is probably a great idea to always make a habit of going to the warm-down (or swim-down) pool to unwind a little before you have to face anyone. This will ensure that some of the emotions may have passed by the time

Mind Training for Swimmers

you have to speak to anyone, and you will be able to remain more in control of your thoughts and feelings. This is better for both yourself *and* anyone you speak to!

So from now on, begin to take responsibility for your thoughts, and become choosy about what you think. This will transform you into a person who *expects the best* at all times, and we all know that we generally *get what we expect.*

Protective Bubble Visualization Method

This method is used to repel negative thoughts directed at you from other people, and it works surprisingly well - as it sends your subconscious a signal that you need protection from negativity. It utilises tailor-made imagery that we discussed in the visualization chapter.

All you do is simply visualize your body surrounded by a *transparent protective bubble,* which is filled with glowing, positive energy. Needless to say, you visualize this so realistically that you can almost *feel* the positive energy inside this bubble.

Then you simply imagine people directing negative comments in your direction - and actually *see* these comments moving towards you and simply bouncing off this impenetrable bubble. Meanwhile, you remain safe and totally unaffected, inside. Once again, it is a very simply technique, but very effective. Try it! It works!

Mind Training for Swimmers

Make Positivity A Way Of Life

Many swimmers seem to think that if they simply have a positive attitude during their swimming meets, they will succeed. But this is not totally correct. To have the best possible chance, you really need to have a positive attitude *all day long, each and every day* – and at the very minimum, during the two weeks before the event began. I suppose what I am saying is that to get the best out of your swimming, you really need to become a positive *person* - that is, if you are not one already!

To be highly successful in swimming, you require a positive outlook *on life in general,* not just during training or meets. Just take a look at any of the great champions, and you will notice they are all generally upbeat, fun people to be around, regardless of whether they are at the pool or not. This is because they have developed a positive attitude to life and everything they do, including swimming, and their results show both in and out of the pool.

It's no secret that people who moan, groan and grumble are rarely successful in the long-term, because negative attitudes simply don't cut it anymore at the highest levels of competition.

It's also interesting that negative people tend to congregate with (or hang around with) other negative people, and the same applies to successful, positive people, who also tend to 'hang out' together.

This is because positive attracts positive, and negative attracts negative. Never forget this. If the people you surround yourself with are negative people, it becomes very difficult to succeed, in swimming or any other area of life.

Mind Training for Swimmers

On the other side of the coin, if you are around positive, upbeat people, generally it will become much easier to achieve better results, both in the pool and out. Needless to say, this means you will attract other positive people, and this can only be good for your swimming career as well.

We can only be as good as the company we keep. This is not to say you should go out and change your friends tomorrow, it's to say that it's important to *work* at being a positive individual. This will make success in the pool much easier, because *things come much easier* to these types of people.

People who are always *down on themselves* generally have things constantly going wrong in their life - and for this to change they must change their attitude, and quickly! Winners are grinners - I'm sure you have heard this saying before, and this really means that *positive people become successful people!*

I once heard that Ian Thorpe believed that he had never *lost* a race in his life – because losing was not coming second, it was getting out of the water *knowing you could have done better.* Using this philosophy, it means that if you have always tried 110% in every race, you have actually won every race you have been in! This is an incredibly powerful mindset that literally allows no place for negative thoughts whatsoever, and one that you could easily try to bring into your current mindset.

Power Words

Mind Training for Swimmers

Remember to put yourself on a mental diet over the next four weeks, and monitor your words, thoughts, statements and especially your favourite sayings for hidden *negatives* - and erase them from your vocabulary forever. There are certain words you simply want to *abolish completely* from your mental computer, never to be uttered again - and replaced with new, positive, upbeat powerful words.

Here are just a few words worth getting rid of, forever. I'm sure you can add to this list.

Useless	Hopeless
Hopeless	I can't...
Never	Lose
What's the use?	No way...
Depressed	Scared
Impossible	Complain
Loser	I can't win...
They're too good....	

You get the general idea...I can't even bear to write any more of these words! These are all words you can do with *less* of in your life.

On the other hand, here is a selection of Power Words that you can never have *enough* of! These are great for creating a powerful vocabulary. Use them and make them a part of your everyday language, thoughts and conversation!

Brilliant	Powerful
Extraordinary	Perfect

Mind Training for Swimmers

Fabulous	Power
Lightning (speed)	Incredible
Believe	Winner
Success	Drive
Motivated	Hyped
Excited	Magnificent
Yes!!!	Great
Unbelievable	Energized
Best	Peak
Personal best	Best ever
Unbeatable	Effortless
Phenomenal	Confident
Courage	Unlimited
Easy	Better
Energy	Amazing
Calm and relaxed	Everything is going perfectly

Just *looking* at those words is motivating and can change your mood! Imagine what they'd do for you if you used them all everyday! So begin today - replacing the negative words and phrases from your vocabulary with power words. To become a champion you must act like one, and this means the way a champion speaks and thinks. If you can learn to *think like a champion,* it will become much easier to succeed - this is a fact of life!

Mind Training for Swimmers

Plus, the bonus to this is that because of their attitude, champions generally excel in *everything* they do, because they go in with the right attitude from the beginning. This means that you get an extra 'payback' for being positive by getting better marks at school, better results at work, becoming more popular, learning new skills more quickly and easily, and simply having a lot more fun in the process!

Begin speaking and thinking the way a champion swimmer would, not like someone who *wants* to be a champion. To become a champion, you must begin thinking like one *right now,* because if you don't, you may never get the chance. Develop a champion's attitude from today onwards, and notice the difference in your results and your life - it will amaze you.

Look For All the Reasons Why You Like The Conditions Today!

A positive state of mind is highly important in both *training and* racing, before you go into the pool. A negative thought pattern encourages you to look for *excuses* for putting in an *average* performance, and this is not what you want. For example, you might find yourself thinking thoughts such as "I don't like this pool", or "I can never beat (Sarah/Peter)" or "the warm-up pool is too crowded", or "John upset me with what he said", etc etc.

This is the *mind looking for things to moan about*. This does not help your performances in the pool at all, in fact it puts the swimmer at a definite disadvantage. The way around this is to *reverse* this negative

Mind Training for Swimmers

way of thinking, and go through a checklist each day as to why you are *looking forward* to swimming today.

This will get you *condition you to being in a positive frame of mind* each and every day, which makes it vastly easier to be positive on the day of a big meet. And needless to say, if you are feeling positive, then you are giving yourself the best possible chance to swim well and *attract any luck* that may be needed. This is why all champions are positive people. Luck is no accident, it magnetizes to people with upbeat attitudes.

Remember, whatever we focus upon, *expands* - this means that if we look for problems, we'll find them - however if we choose to look for the positive aspects, we'll find those as well. It's completely your choice! Choose wisely.

Never Criticise Yourself After Races

Once a race is over, make sure you don't take this an opportunity to abuse yourself mentally. Sure, analyse the way you swam and look for ways to improve, but *keep it positive* - you must support yourself mentally, because if you don't, who else is going to? There are plenty of people around who would be only too happy to put you down, so don't bother doing it yourself!

Abusing yourself only pulls down your confidence and will never direct you towards your goals. You must become your own personal *cheer squad* - motivating yourself with encouragement, affirmations and positive thoughts.

Mind Training for Swimmers

There is no need to show everyone how you feel, but deep down you must *know and believe* that you are a *fabulous person who deserves success*. This is the way a champion thinks, though they may never actually tell anyone that.

Champions always have a fabulous self-image - they never put themselves down (jokingly yes, but seriously, never) and they will not allow anyone else to put them down, either. If someone criticizes them (un-constructively), they simply choose *not to mentally accept* those comments, and physically move into a more positive environment, around people who are more supportive.

So never make the mistake of berating yourself - plenty of others will be happy to do that for you, so boost yourself up and come back stronger than ever.

Do You Have The Approach Of A Winner?

It's important to constantly monitor how you are thinking about an approaching meet. Your mental approach and general attitude to the meet can often be a *complete giveaway* as to how you will perform.

Here is a description of the *essence* of the negative and the positive approaches to swimming - the fact is that most people are neither *completely* one nor the other, but usually somewhere in between, combining a little of both. However, reading through these will illustrate the pitfalls and help you to avoid the negative approach - and show you what's required to be successful.

Mind Training for Swimmers

Firstly, here is the completely negative approach, of a swimmer who would need to make a major shift in attitude to get any results.

The Completely Negative Approach
(To Be Avoided At All Costs)

The negative swimmer never looks forward to meets, because they represent stress to them - as they constantly worry about everything that could go wrong. Often they don't enjoy their training either, finding it boring and hard work.

At meets they worry about their competitors, and what their coach or family will think if they don't perform. The meets are absolutely no fun at all, but more of an *ordeal* - mainly because they are in a state of fear before their races. If they don't swim well in the heats, they're often secretly relieved that they do not have to swim in a final later on. Despite this, they blame themselves for not being good enough, constantly going over bad results again and again in their minds. This can often make them feel depressed for the rest of the week.

When they swim well, they do not always experience joy from the result, as they usually feel that they should have performed that way "ages ago". This is the outlook of a swimmer who needs to make a *major* change in their attitude for their results to change.

The Completely Positive Approach
(This Is What We Should All Aspire To Have!)

Mind Training for Swimmers

The successful swimmer looks forward to meets, because they represent a fun time plus an *opportunity* to show how good they are. They also enjoy training, because they find it satisfying and are motivated to tune themselves up for the next meet.

They only think positively about future meets and races, and how *well* they may go in them. They swim purely for themselves, not worrying too much about what anyone else thinks, because *what they think about themselves* is far more important.

They never worry about who is in their races, because they only focus on their *own* swim, not anyone else's. Whenever they perform well in a race they *use* this confidence to boost themselves up for the next race. However, if they do not perform well, it's quickly forgotten because they *choose to focus on the next race,* instead of dwelling in the past about something they cannot change.

The entire meet is generally a fun experience - being with friends, enjoying the challenge of competing, succeeding and at times failing. If they go through a bad patch of races, which all good swimmers do at times, it simply *doubles* their determination, and they always end up coming out on top. This is the approach of a positive swimmer, destined for success.

Do you recognize yourself in either of these descriptions? The odds are you probably noticed that you might have some characteristics from a little of *both*, but hopefully far more from the positive approach! If not, you'd better get to work!

Mind Training for Swimmers

I'm sure you can also think of swimmers who would fit into both of these descriptions. Read through this positive approach regularly, and work towards achieving that attitude. This attitude cannot help but bring strong results eventually.

Avoid Negative People

In order to keep your mind positive before races, it's best to be with positive people who will support you and whom you can relax with. On the other side of the coin, it's also best to *avoid* those who criticize you or try and bring you down - this mainly applies to *before* races, but this is also not bad advice for life in general!

We can only rise to the level of the company we keep, and if you are spending most of your time with negative people, it will have a major effect on your outlook, and your results. Seek the company of fun positive people, and this will be much more beneficial to your chances of success.

Criticism Is A Sign Of Success!

Always remember that if people seem to be criticizing you a lot for no apparent reason, then this is a sign that you are getting closer to success! Jealousy and envy inevitably get directed towards people who begin to shine above the crowd - and so you must learn to *expect it, and ignore it,* if you wish to be successful. This is what all champions had to learn to *rise above* in order to make it to the top.

Mind Training for Swimmers

When you draw criticism from others - which is purely designed to de-rail your dreams, usually by jealous competitors (or their parents or friends!), simply pat yourself on the back and say "I must be on the way to the top!"

Do not spend one moment worrying about it - there is absolutely nothing you can do about it, unless you wish to stop succeeding, and you're certainly not going to give them the pleasure of that option! Just ignore them and stay out of their company, and remain with your true friends and allies.

The Last Word

Before I finish this chapter, I hope I've emphasized enough that a negative attitude is the only thing that I can *de-rail* the powerful techniques such as visualization and affirmations.

If you use these techniques and blend them with a *positive* attitude, then the sky really is the limit - because you will be getting everything possible out of the techniques. Of course, there is much more to discuss yet, however the bottom line is that a positive attitude is an absolute must - there is NO possibility of winning without it!

So begin your four- week mental diet today, cleansing every negative thought from your mind until you are left with a positive thought pattern. Do this using the Delete and Detachment Methods, and the Affirmation Technique, as well as any other methods that may have struck a chord with you.

Mind Training for Swimmers

Here is your summary for this chapter, containing three compulsory mental exercises for your Mental Training Program – but, as you will notice with some relief, none of which are the slightest bit time-consuming whatsoever.

Summary

- Mental Training Program:

  Notice, cancel, and replace all negative *thoughts and statements* as soon as they arise.

- Mental Training Program:

  Watch the words you choosing to use for the next 4 weeks - are they positive? Replace negative words and statements with more positive ones.

- Mental Training Program:

  Don't get *emotionally involved* in any negative thoughts, just let them wither and die from lack of attention.

- At meets, ask yourself the question *"what's great about this?"* And then you allow your mind to come up with the answers - and soon you have a whole bunch of great reasons why things will go well for you today.

- It is *essential* for all budding champions to work at being positive virtually *all day long* (not just the day of the meet), choosing not to focus or dwell upon negative thoughts of any kind.

Mind Training for Swimmers

- It's not the *negative thought* or the *person* who annoys us - it is our *reaction* to them. Choose <u>not</u> to react, and you take away their power over you forever.

- Be especially careful to be positive when you would *normally feel down;* eg, after a bad race. Don't let emotion get mixed with negative thoughts!

- Become known as 'the machine' who never gets down about anything, and never lets anything get in their way from what they want. Eventually competitors will give up trying to unsettle you, and they will become quite psyched out by your mental strength.

- Keep your mind *on the goal*, and *off the obstacles*, using tunnel vision before races.

- If you find yourself 'stressing out' at a meet, begin monitoring your thoughts, and checking that you are focusing upon positives (such as affirmations) and not thinking about the 'uncontrollables'.

- Work at becoming a positive person, because generally they become successful people. Be around positive people as much as possible.

- Watch constantly at meets to see if you're worrying about uncontrollables - they need to be erased immediately, or the focus of your thoughts changed to something more positive. Don't allow these to take a hold of your

Mind Training for Swimmers

thoughts before races, they are the swimmer's greatest enemy!

- Avoid negative people, or anyone who pressures you, before races. Be with people you can relax with, otherwise find some quiet time alone.

- Do you have the approach of a winner? Constantly monitor your attitude to meets.

- Your attitude at training each day will determine the results you achieve at meets. Train positively and with a purpose, keeping your eyes only on your goal.

- Each day, on the way home from training, think of what you did best in the pool that day, and run images of this through your mind all over again. Do this every day, to give yourself a boost of positivity and motivation.

CHAPTER 7

Everything You Should Know About Goals

To achieve anything in life, you must have a goal or direction. For swimmers, this is also very important - a swimmer without a goal is like a boat without a sail, drifting aimlessly. Goals *get you motivated* to get up and work towards what it is you really want to achieve in your life.

Most good coaches these days help their swimmers to work out what their goals are - so it is important to talk to your coach regarding these. When working out your goals, it's important that they are *big* enough to excite and motivate you, but *small* enough for you to feel that you can still achieve them.

For instance, if you were setting yourself a goal of taking 10 seconds off your PB, this may be very exciting, but you may eventually lose motivation and get frustrated trying to achieve this goal because it may seem too big to achieve in one go.

It's much better instead to make a big goal like this your 'long-term goal', and then split it into smaller 'short term goals' which eventually lead to you achieving your ultimate destination. Write down some smaller, achievable goals, like taking 2 seconds off your PB each

Mind Training for Swimmers

time, until you reach your ultimate 10 second mark. This is the best way to make goals.

Goals must also be definite and specific, and something that you really WANT. They should excite you. If you're trying to achieve something that really doesn't motivate you, or if the goal is *not specific enough* - such as something like 'I want to improve my time', you're eventually going to get tired of it and give it away. Your goal must excite you, and it must also be something *definite* - like a specific time, or a specific event you want to win.

We rarely succeed at things we cannot hold a clear mental picture of, or things we do not enjoy or aren't motivated about. So always aim for something definite that really *means* something to you!

Goals should also be written down in your mental training exercise book, so you can look at them regularly, make changes if needed and tick them off as you achieve them. Writing them down is very important, as it cements them in your mind and makes them more real and believable to you.

However, keep your goals secret, except to your closest allies, as you do not want to draw criticism from others who may criticize your goal. Jealousy will always make others try and stop you achieving what you want. It's much better to keep your goals secret until you have achieved them, and *then* you can let them know if you wish, or (even better!) let them find out about it from someone else.

Also, be prepared for your goals to possibly change along the way. This may *not* happen, but you must also be prepared for it in case it does. For instance, you may find that you're moving towards your goal quicker and easier than you expected, and you might have to make some more goals along the way to keep yourself motivated.

Or, you may find that another *event* such as your butterfly might be getting stronger and slowly taking over as your 'favourite' event, and so you might decide to change your goals towards that event.

The important thing is to change your goals if you feel they *need* changing - don't struggle on if you feel that you are heading in the wrong direction. Please note that I am not talking about quitting every time you feel down, because *every* champion feels down along the way to achieving his or her dreams. I mean that if you and your coach feel that you need a change of direction, then make the change - then go for it, and let nothing get it your way.

If things go as you *had* been hoping (and even if the progress is slow), keep on with the goal and never let go until you've achieved it. Persistence will pay off if you hang in there long enough, the key is to be passionate about your goal, and this means you will move mountains to achieve it.

So if you don't have any goals written down yet, go and do this now in your exercise book before you read on any further. Put your dreams down in black and white.

Here is your summary for this chapter, which does not contain any compulsory mental exercises for your Mental Training Program.

Mind Training for Swimmers

Summary

- Write down your goals but keep them secret except for your   closest allies. Make sure they are
what you really *want*, and that they are achievable - but also big enough to motivate you.

- Make the major goal big enough to truly motivate you, but small enough to keep you interested in it.

- Be prepared to change your goal if circumstances change.

Mind Training for Swimmers

CHAPTER 8

The Zone

One of the most powerful mental states in sport (but also one of the *least-known* in swimming) is the mental state known as 'the zone'. This is the mental state, which produces super-human performances, amazing times and winning streaks. It is a well-known term in many other sports, but I have discovered that most swimmers have never heard of it.

Any swimmer or athlete who is in this mental state is virtually unbeatable at their respective level of competition - and when at the elite level, you often witness world records being well and truly smashed.

This is one of the techniques, which will literally blast your competition out of the water if you can perfect it, so it is definitely worth practicing and perfecting.

A swimmer who is 'in the zone' experiences an unusual feeling of *effortless power*, almost as if their body was powered by a turbo-charged engine, and their body glides and cuts through the water with awesome power.

Mind Training for Swimmers

This sensation is almost eerie, as you almost feel like you are 'one with the water', rather than being a swimmer *in* the water. The other strange sensation is that this incredible performance does *not feel as if the actual swimmer is controlling it!* In fact, they often report feeling as if they weren't responsible for the swim at all - as if their body was being *guided and directed* by a more powerful force (and this is *exactly* what is actually happening).

Almost every swimmer at some stage in their career has experienced this feeling to some extent, and then wondered afterwards "how did I do that?" This is the mystery that surrounds this mental state called *the zone* - why does it appear so fleetingly, and then disappear just as quickly as it came? And most of all, why can't we access this mental state all the time?

So what *is* this powerful force that is guiding the body during this period? The answer is the sleeping giant that resides inside all human beings, and the source of all bodily movement which contains all your past swimming experiences. Yes, it's your subconscious mind!

When a swimmer is 'zoning', their *conscious* mind (our normally busy, chattering mind) becomes unusually quiet, allowing their more powerful *subconscious* to run their performance on 'auto-pilot', in the same way a computer runs software.

This allows their strokes to flow much easier, effortlessly increasing speed and power in a way that could never be matched by conscious thought. This means that when you are in the zone, you have *virtually no thought going through your mind whatsoever*, your body is

Mind Training for Swimmers

just swimming on automatic-pilot, powered directly by your subconscious.

This is *not* to say that your body is swimming without instruction - on the contrary, it is simply getting its instructions from a far more powerful and reliable source. By thinking zero thoughts, this also takes away the pressure of *expectation.* As soon as the pressure is taken off, this is the time when most swimmers become capable of reaching the zone and achieving something special in the pool.

The zone is often achieved when you are NOT intending to swim a particularly special time, and the pressure is off. This is why (in meets) it can sometimes be helpful to pretend that you are *not* the favourite in a race, *even if you really are* - as this may allow you to relax more and make 'the zone' more reachable for you. This is something you will have to experiment with, as of course, some swimmers perform better when the pressure is <u>on</u> them. (If you find this is the case, then you probably won't need to do this). It seems, however, that the majority of swimmers seem to perform better when under *less* stress of public expectation.

This is the thing about mental training which makes it unique for everyone, with many techniques (such as this one) requiring the swimmer to find their own particular way of utilising it most effectively for themselves.

So is there one particular way to get into the zone? No, there are several ways, but because everyone is different, you must experiment to find the method that best suits you.

Mind Training for Swimmers

It is recommended that you try this at intervals in your daily training. Not all the time, as you also need to consciously work on things such as technique in your training, but every so often, do a set where you are trying to access the zone. (It almost seems strange writing that line 'trying to access the zone' - as the very key to getting into the zone is NOT to try – but I think you understand what I mean!).

Here's a short mental checklist when you are about to try a set 'in the zone'.

- Clear your mind of all thought just before the race or set. Thoughts only get in the way, and keeps your conscious mind involved in your swimming, which is not what you want. The clearer your mind can be, the more easily your subconscious mind can click in to run your entire performance.

- Pay absolutely no attention to anything around you except the blocks and your race. Once again, the last thing we want is for your conscious mind to be involved, so just allow yourself to 'go within' and do not think about the surroundings (or anything) whatsoever.

- Allow your body to swim on 'automatic pilot' without thought. During this time just allow your body to be *guided*, rather than directed, by your mind. This allows your subconscious to take the driver's seat, which is the way to swimming in the zone. This, of course, seems to go against all of the 'normal' ways we would approach anything -

Mind Training for Swimmers

thinking about what we are doing is such a natural occurrence to most of us, but the key is *not to*. If anything, try and *feel* the swim, rather than orchestrating it. If you wish, you can even experiment with thinking about something completely different altogether, while you are swimming (though best to practice this in training first, rather than meets), purely to distract your conscious mind from focusing upon the swim (as its your subconscious that we need to run the performance, not your conscious mind).

Remember that it's difficult to get into the zone when you are *trying* to do it - it usually happens when you least expect it. When you release yourself from the pressure of expectation (from yourself or others), your mind directs your body's performance as it truly wishes. So the best way is to use *effortless effort*.

Do not allow your mind to project *backward or forward in time* - just 'be here now' and allow yourself to swim as you have been trained. The present will never hold any fear for you. Only the past or the future creates the fears. Remind yourself that there is only *now*, as this reduces stress as well as helping you reach the zone.

When you are at a meet, don't worry about whether you will swim well enough, just know that you have already put in the time and the training, and that the result will take care of itself. This can help prevent you from *over trying*. Just relax and let it happen. This is what I would like you to practice thinking in training, until it becomes automatic.

Practicing getting into the zone is definitely something you should only practice in training, until you have perfected it enough to try in the meets. You don't want to go trying this for the first time in a big race, wait until you are getting a handle on it first. But remember, do not practice this every single set of your training, as you also have other things such as technique to work on as well.

However, I highly recommend practicing this in your training over the next eight weeks, as mastering this mental state consistently produces first-class results. So do not underestimate the zone - it will bring you better performances than you could ever imagine.

Ian Thorpe once mentioned that his mindset was as *neutral* as possible while he swam, and that he simply allowed his body to do what it knows best. This is a classic way to reach the zone - by simply surrendering to the swimming control centre - your subconscious mind, which runs the body's performances automatically - and simply allowing it to *instinctively run the performance,* rather than trying to consciously orchestrate or direct it, as one might in training.

Another Way To Click Into 'The Zone'

Being in the zone means that your body is functioning at peak efficiency, getting the *best possible result using the least possible amount of energy*. This means that when your stroking rhythm is at its best, you will often *automatically* click right into the zone.

If you work on attaining your best possible rhythm and stroking efficiency (rather than focusing purely upon speed) often your speed will occur naturally and automatically.

By focusing upon your *rhythm* in training, you may actually attain more speed than if you focused upon speed itself. This is almost one of those Catch-22 situations - and very much like the Zen principle *'Less is more'*. The less you focus upon speed, the more speed you will get. This principle works in golf, tennis and many other sports as well. But once again, the place to practice this is *not* in the meets, it's in training - this is the place to master it, so that you can unleash it in the meets.

So try working on your *stroking rhythm* in training, as this is a *physical* way of getting into the zone, rather than the mental methods we've discussed earlier. But don't expect it to happen immediately - if it were easy, everyone would be a great swimmer!

Here is your summary for this chapter, which does not contain any compulsory mental exercises for your Mental Training Program.

Summary

- Practice getting into the zone in your training over the following 2 months (unless you have a meet in a week's time, of course). This will be time well invested.

Mind Training for Swimmers

• Practice 'being in the moment', not projecting your mind to the past or future when swimming at meets. Do this by clearing your mind of all thought, and allowing your body to swim on autopilot.

• Practice reaching the zone in training through a more physical method, by working on the *rhythm and efficiency* of your strokes instead of focusing purely upon speed. This will lead to accessing more speed for your races anyway.

• Mentally take some pressure off yourself and see if this helps you to reach the zone more easily.

• Remember the harder you *try* to get into the zone, the further you move away from it!

CHAPTER 9

Conditioning Your Mind To Handle Pain

Pain is something each swimmer must learn to overcome on the journey to success - and every swimmer has a different level of ability to deal with it.

The human body is designed to be able to overcome extreme pain - as it contains a natural painkiller called morphine, which is one of the strongest (hospital-strength) painkillers in the world. This morphine is automatically called upon by our subconscious if we experience sudden extreme pain, such as during a sudden major accident - and it instantly prevents any pain being experienced. Many accident victims who have had limbs severed report feeling *absolutely nothing at all* at the actual time of the accident - as their subconscious mind instantly *anaesthetized* (or numbed) the affected area.

We can also access this ability using particular techniques that 'trick' the subconscious mind into releasing morphine into our system, to kill the pain. It's a 100% natural and legal painkiller!

Mind Training for Swimmers

It's important to know that pain is not necessarily always a *bad* thing, it signals that you are getting towards the business end of your swim and that this is when your competitors are feeling the pain as well. However, pain can become an emotional issue as well, and when we get *overly* emotional about the pain, it increases further pain . So whenever you experience pain, try to deal with it as *unemotionally* as possible without allowing your mind to exaggerate how it feels (and yes, this *is* possible!).

There are various methods to dealing with pain, however as each swimmer is different, you must experiment to find out which methods suit you best.

Delaying The Pain

I find that one of the best ways is to practice mentally *delaying the pain.* You see, in your mind you already know *the exact time in the race* your body is going to begin hurting. Believe it or not, after a while this becomes a conditioned response or 'reflex action' where your body *automatically begins to hurt* because it knows that you happen to be at this stage of the race! I have found that by getting swimmers to practice *delaying the pain* by 20 metres in their visualizations, they could slowly but surely reduce the amount of pain they felt in races. I have even worked with swimmers who have managed to *completely overcome* pain when racing.

You do this by taking yourself through a *course* of daily visualizations, the first of which may take anywhere from one to several

Mind Training for Swimmers

weeks before you begin to sense that you are ready to move onto Stage 2 of the course. Here's how you begin, with Stage 1.

When you are visualizing your swim each day, you imagine the exact point in the race (or training) where you normally feel the pain - for instance, this point seems to often be around the 320m mark for a lot of 400m swimmers.

However, instead of imagining that you are experiencing the pain at this particular stage, you mentally 'see' yourself continuing to swim pain-free until you reach a point 20 metres further down the pool. At this point you *briefly* imagine the pain beginning to hit as you swim, followed by imagining your body *glowing radiantly* with bright gold or yellow light (which the subconscious interprets as energy), which quickly begins to evaporate the pain. At this point you imagine yourself rapidly *moving through the pain* until it completely *disappears* - as you finish the race strongly and powerfully, feeling great.

So during Stage 1, not only does the pain 'hit' 20 metres *later* than normal, you also imagine the pain being *evaporated by the radiant glowing light,* which makes it quickly disappear - these are the three key points of this stage 1 exercise. Once you begin to feel that this is happening in your actual training and races, it is time to move on to Stage 2.

The visualization for Stage 2 is almost exactly the same, except that you imagine your body experiencing the pain another 20m *further* into the race than in Stage 1 (i.e., 20m further than last time, and 40m further than the *original* time the pain used to hit). Once again the pain

Mind Training for Swimmers

is evaporated by the radiant glowing energy in your body, so that it does not make any great mental impression upon you.

Keep doing Stage 2 of the visualization until you feel that your mind is beginning to accept this new 'program' and you are beginning to see similar results in your training or races - and then move onto Stage 3.

Stage 3 is exactly the same visualization, except a further 20m once again delays the pain - and you simply continue to move through these stages one at a time, until you feel that you can eventually swim your races virtually pain-free.

Please note that this method works far better than trying to imagine *one stage only* (of no pain whatsoever) - this seems to be much more difficult for the mind to accept, it's far better to condition your mind *to delay* the pain first.

These stages *can* also be achieved without proper visualization, though it is a little more difficult to get the same results. This is done by simply *consciously deciding* (over and over again in your mind) that you now have a new point in the race where you will feel the pain. This method may take quite a lot longer to achieve the results, however.

I also have a specific Mind Training for Swimmers - 'Overcoming Pain' CD if you are interested in this, specially designed to help overcome the pain of practice and racing, which you take a look at here: http://www.swimpsychology.com/pain_CD.php3

Mind Training for Swimmers

More Pain Relief

Another successful method is to remind yourself (when experiencing pain in training and races) that you are not *in* pain, you are simply *moving through* the pain. This is *a signal* to your mind that the pain is only a *temporary process*, instead of resigning yourself to the fact that you are stuck with increasing pain as you swim. There is a big difference between these two approaches, and it can make a huge difference between the ways you react to the pain.

Another method is to use the pain as *a trigger,* signalling to your mind that your race is nearly over, and to automatically speed up to finish strongly. After practicing this around 20 times, it can become an *automatic response* each time you begin to feel the pain hit. It is amazing how you can condition your mind and body to have *automatic responses* to certain triggers - including pain.

Some swimmers also handle the pain better by reminding themselves that their competitors are also hurting, and this makes them more determined to handle the pain better than their competitors.

So experiment with some of these approaches and find the method that best suits you - your results will tell you which works best for you. Here is your summary for this chapter, which does not contain any compulsory mental exercises for your Mental Training Program.

Summary

- Pain can be overcome naturally using your mind, and the natural painkillers present in your body.

Mind Training for Swimmers

- Practice *delaying* the pain 20 metres at a time, until it eventually has little affect upon you.

- Remember to move *through* the pain, instead of being *in* it.

- Remind yourself that your competitors are also in pain, and that you will handle it better.

- Set up a mental *trigger-response* where pain instantly signals to your mind that it is time to speed up and finish the race.

Mind Training for Swimmers

CHAPTER 10

What Is Your Peak Emotional State?

Please note: To do this exercise, I highly recommend buying an exercise book which is purely devoted to your mental training, and compiling important lists (such as this exercise) in it. The more you learn about *yourself*, the more powerful you will be in the pool - and this exercise is one of several which will increase your awareness of your own mind and body, in order to extract more from your performances in future.

Other exercises I will mention later in the 'lists' chapter will be very handy to keep in this book as well, to take with you at meets - for times when you need some extra help or a boost of mental power.

This exercise book can become your own *secret cheer squad,* a stockpile of inspiration that no-one else knows about - and keep it hidden from all except your closest allies! To ensure your privacy you might even want to put some boring obscure name on the front of the book (so no-one will be curious to look inside) and place the

Mind Training for Swimmers

information *in the middle or the back* of the book, so it stays well hidden away from prying eyes.

What Mood Creates Your Best Performance?

You may not have noticed it before, but most of the time you are in a *particular mood* every time you swim at your best. This particular mood consistently provides strong results for you, all you need to do is find out what it is.

You also have a particular mood, which consistently delivers your *worst* performances; and it's also important to know what this is as well - so you can avoid it as much as possible before races!

Moods (or emotional states) are an inescapable fact for every human being and vital to your chances when swimming important meets. Emotional states are somewhat *less* important in training - for instance it's more difficult to get as *emotionally charged* in training as you might in a big meet.

Every swimmer possesses their own personal 'winning mood' - but most are unaware of this or know what it is. Simply *knowing* information such as this puts you in the driver's seat, and ahead of your competitors! However, the only problem with this is there are *hundreds* of different moods and emotional states - so how do we find out which one is our *peak emotional state*? For this purpose, I have narrowed the huge range of moods down to only 4 main ones, which I believe are the most important for swimming (and sport in general).

Mind Training for Swimmers

These moods include, but are not limited to:

| Hyped & excited | Calm & focused |
| Nervousness | Anger |

Once you know your own peak emotional state, you can try to get yourself *into* that particular mood before important races. The way to discover your peak emotional state is to create a Mood Chart, like the one below. This allows you to map out what your highest (and lowest) performing mood is, over the course of 20-30 races.

All you do is simply write down how you *feel emotionally* before each and every race, and then rate each swim afterwards on a scale of 1 to 10, as to how good the performance was. So (for example only) you might have a list of races that look like this:

Mood Chart				
Date	Emotion Before Race	Performance Level	Best	Worst
4th March	Nervous	6	-	-
5th March	Hyped/Excited	9	*	-
11th March	Angry	5	-	*
12th March	Hyped/Excited	8.5	*	-
18th March	Calm/Relaxed	7	-	-
19th March	Hyped/Excited	9	*	-
Etc				

Mind Training for Swimmers

As this example shows, this swimmer's three best performances were when they were hyped and excited, and their worst result came on the day that they were angry about something. This is just an example, as other swimmers might find that this is the exact opposite for them, as everyone is different. This is highly valuable information worth knowing before you go into any race.

So, if the chart above shows that this swimmer is best when hyped and excited before a race, they might use motivational music from a CD player or iPod to help them get hyped-up and into their peak emotional state. As the chart also suggests that anger is their worst mood of all, they should probably avoid getting emotionally upset or angry before races - this could mean staying away from people who might irritate them before they go out for a race!

If a swimmer discovers that they are best when they are calm and relaxed before races, they could use relaxation techniques and /or music to help get them in their peak emotional state. For swimmers who swim best when they are angry (and there are some of them out there!) they can actually practice looking for reasons to get angry, such as pretending that everyone in the race thinks that they are the worst swimmer on the block, etc.

Let me point out once again that every single swimmer is different - you have to find out your own peak emotional state, and only *you* can do it. By recording this information for about 20-30 races, it will reveal your personal moods, which will deliver your best (and worst) performances.

Mind Training for Swimmers

The more information you can discover about *yourself,* the better swimmer you will be. Knowing yourself inside out means you will know exactly how to mentally approach stressful situations, meets and problems that may arise. It is a worthwhile exercise that only takes a few seconds at a time to compile after each race.

Avoid Emotional Ups and Downs

In the week before an important meet, it's highly preferable to ensure you keep your emotions in harmony and equilibrium. Basically this means - stay happy!

Major swings in mood, especially those triggered by negative events such as arguments, personal problems, confrontations etc can have a disastrous effect on your performance - as they deplete your mental and physical energy which you need for your races.

The whole emphasis in the week before a meet (or even for 2 weeks, for the biggest events) should be on keeping your life on a nice *constant and harmonious straight line* rather than the highs and lows of emotional mood swings. Any major personal issues looming before meets are best either:

- Diffused immediately
- Ignored completely, or
- Postponed, and taken care of *after the meet is over*

Be very aware that emotions are highly delicate and can be easily upset, and must be carefully and gently nursed through the week before

Mind Training for Swimmers

each meet, so that you will be at your physical and mental best on the day.

You do not want to expend too much mental energy before the meet, as this too must be 'tapered' just like some swimmers do with their physical workouts, so that you will be in peak condition for the meet. Here is your summary for this chapter, which does not contain any compulsory mental exercises for your Mental Training Program.

Summary

- Create a Mood Chart in your exercise book to find out your Peak Emotional State (and try to get yourself into that winning mood before each race, using music and other tools). Also consider discovering your peak sleeping patterns and foods to bring you your best performances in the pool.

- Try and keep your emotions on an even keel in the week before any meet, avoiding anything which might create negative fluctuations in your emotions. Either solve potential problems quickly, or postpone them until after the meet is over. Taper your emotions as well as your training.

Mind Training for Swimmers

"I saw my name: THOMAS, Petria. Saw my time, 57.72. Saw the number one next to them. I'd done it. Me! Petria Thomas, Olympic champion. The feeling inside was one of pure, utter joy. Excitement, disbelief, relief, happiness, amazement, the whole works. I'd worked so hard. I'd gone through so much, privately, publicly. I'd lost faith in myself and found it again. I'd sometimes stopped believing that I could do it and that I had a purpose in life. I'd come through the darkness, and this, this moment, was the sweetest, most amazing light there could possibly be. I was alive and loving it!"

Petria Thomas, Athens Olympic Gold Medallist

Mind Training for Swimmers

CHAPTER 11

Dealing With Pressure And Expectation

All good swimmers must face the spotlight of expectation from others at some stage in their careers. This can undoubtedly exert extra pressure on you to perform, which can cause anxiety and affect your swim if you are not careful.

One effective way (of the several methods) to deal with expectation is to 'downplay' the whole situation - this means to *keep reducing its importance* until you begin to feel more relaxed about it. Actually, when you think about it, this is simply putting things into their *proper perspective* so that you see the situation more clearly for what it really is. For instance, many people in the world are wondering how they are going to be able to afford to *eat* this week - and here we are, worried about a swim meet! Now *that's* perspective.

A good way to do this is to ask yourself some questions. For instance, you might ask yourself "Am I swimming in front of a huge

Mind Training for Swimmers

television audience of 100 million people this weekend?" and the answer is (usually) NO.

Then you might ask yourself a few more questions: "Do I have multi-million dollar contracts that are riding on this meet?" NO!

"Will anyone remember this race in 5 years time?" NO!

"Do most of the world's population *care* whether I swim well or not?" NO!

"Will the human race *end* if I don't win at this meet?" NO!

And this continues, until you realize an important point. Just how important is this meet after all? The answer is - not really so important at all! Certainly not important enough to bother staying awake at night worrying about it! So put the race into perspective. Don't sweat the small stuff. Most of the time the race will not be anywhere *near* as important as you think it is.

Take The Pressure Off If You're Feeling the Heat

If you are at a meet and find yourself having major trouble with nerves, and not coping with the pressure, try taking some time out and go outside and have a look at *real* life going on. People talking and having fun, kids playing, the peace and tranquillity of nature...all these things will continue to go on *regardless* of how you perform in the pool.

It doesn't *matter* how important it may all seem to your teammates, the coaches, the parents and the friends - the fact is...life will go on anyway. Swimming is not a person's *whole* life, it's simply a *part* of their life. Yes, even for the swimming champions of the world.

Mind Training for Swimmers

There are many other aspects to life, which are just as important, if not *more* important.

Keep in mind that every person you see at the swim meets *also* have other more important aspects of their life than swimming, just like you. The race is not life or death. It is simply…swimming, which even at the highest level, is simply a sport.

Remind yourself of this if the pressure gets too much for you. (Also, keep in mind the 'black curtain' visualization mentioned in the visualization chapter).

You Can Have Anything You Want As Long As You Don't Need It

Has it ever seemed that the harder you try, the further away from your goal you become? Swimmers often experience this whose desire to achieve a major goal becomes so all consuming that *they have trouble thinking about anything else.* When this happens it often creates the situation where, much to their frustration, the goal appears to be moving further away from them instead of getting closer.

Whilst it's important to focus upon your goals, it's also essential to allow yourself to have a mental *break* from the goal as well. Otherwise your mind simply gets tired of focusing on the same thing all the time.

A sure way of knowing when your mind is tired is *when you feel that you really are beginning to dislike swimming,* or are simply *not motivated at all to train or race* - that is the signal to take some time off

Mind Training for Swimmers

or do something quite different. Once you feel refreshed from taking a break, you will come back with loads of enthusiasm and motivation.

When we obsess or focus too much on what we want, it actually *drives our goal further away from us,* because it takes away our physical and mental energy.

The key is to relax when you are swimming, allow your body to do what it has been trained to do, and *trust* that this will be enough to succeed. Don't worry about your performance too much when you are outside of the pool, just let your body do the talking *in* the pool.

A swimmer I worked with was so obsessed with making a particular time for the Nationals that his times actually began to go in the opposite direction! He was focusing upon the goal *too much*, which was taking his attention away from other important issues, such as technique, training, etc. On top of this, he was stressed out before every swim attempt, and each time he *didn't* achieve the time, he felt more and more emotionally drained and frustrated.

So what I told him to do was to *forget about the time,* and just focus upon his technique and training. He found this took the pressure off and allowed him to relax. You might guess what happened a few weeks later - he *made* the time he had set himself. As soon as he took the *focus off* what he desperately wanted, his mind and body could simply relax and allow him to do it. Afterwards he felt that achieving his goal wasn't so hard after all, in fact, in the end it had felt quite *effortless. That is the way to achieve a goal.*

Mind Training for Swimmers

Do You Try Too Hard?

This brings us to the subject of *trying too hard* in races. I am not talking about going into races *without* trying, quite the opposite - we can get more from our mind and body if we just *allow* ourselves to do what it is we've been trained for, instead of *over-trying*.

It's important to have an *intention* when you race, such as achieving a certain time, but these thoughts must only occur *before* (and never during) the race. Once you are in the race, you just allow your body to go into 'automatic pilot' and allow yourself to do what you have set out to do, and what your body has been trained for. (For a lot more on this subject, see 'The Zone').

This is the attitude of champions - they have *complete faith* that everything will work out just as it should. This is *not* to say that they don't go through times of doubt - everyone experiences these at times, however champions quickly discard the doubts and replace them with positive thoughts.

And needless to say, they've also put in the work in training, so that they have *every reason* to feel confident in their races!

Do You Stress Out At Meets?

So many swimmers train brilliantly and then find that at meets they feel highly nervous, full of doubt and low in confidence.

One thing you *can* do at a meet to control these feelings is *control that upon which you are choosing to focus* - are you worrying

Mind Training for Swimmers

needlessly about 'uncontrollables', things about which you simply can do nothing?

Watch for this closely at meets, by simply noticing *if* you are worrying, and also whether these things you are focusing upon are *beyond your control* - which they generally are. Basically I am saying you need to 'observe your thoughts', as this actual process can help to overcome stress all by itself, by moving your focus from your future races. Whenever you notice negative thoughts going through your mind, use the Delete Method and *cancel them out*, or simply shut them out completely by reciting some positive affirmations to yourself, over and over again.

Your thoughts are the one thing you CAN control, never believe that you are a prisoner to your own mind. *You control your mind. It doesn't control you.* Most stress is *self-induced* - so simply don't allow your mind to think stressful thoughts before races, this is the one sure way to stay in control and prevent 'stressing out'.

By controlling what you choose to think, you are going to the very source of your stress and 'nipping it in the bud' before it can affect you. One of the best ways to prevent stressful thoughts is to distract or change them to something else - it doesn't matter what the subject is, as long it's something which is relaxing for you. Even thinking about *funny experiences, friends, or weird and wonderful subjects* can be a good distraction and relaxant.

Remember that you are always the master of your own destiny. Think of big races as a chance to show your superiority in the pressure

Mind Training for Swimmers

situations, because *undoubtedly your competitors will be feeling the pressure as well.*

Know that it's actually possible to *beat a faster swimmer*, simply by *handling the pressure* of the big swim better than they do. If a faster swimmer is swimming with thoughts of *fear of the big occasion*, they will not put in a great time - even if they'd been doing world records in training! Never forget this.

So it no longer becomes how *fast* your competitors are, but *how well can they handle the pressure?* This means that if you can become adept at handling pressure in races, you will be able to come out ahead in the big races that really count. Handling pressure is probably more important than being the swimmer who has done the best times in training during that week, because training times are one thing, but times in finals races are definitely another.

Ignore Reputations

The reputation of a competitor can only affect you if you *choose to allow it.* Reputations actually mean absolutely nothing, as they only point to things that have been achieved in the *past* – and have absolutely nothing to do with how they will swim *today.*

Great times swum in the *past* do not mean that your competitor will be able to achieve those heights again now, in the present. So ignore what your competitors have done in the past, and treat them purely on how they swim *today.*

Mind Training for Swimmers

When you read the next topic coming up you will realize that it actually doesn't matter *how* your competitors swim, because it will only be *your own swim* you will want to focus upon anyway.

Of course, if you happen to have a reputation of your own, this is a completely different situation - and can be very handy! Whether it's in the meets or moving up to a new age group, it can be of great help to have some kind of reputation as a swimmer, as it may strike some fear into your competitors - especially those who don't know you personally but have *heard* of your performances. Even though YOU know that reputations mean nothing, it doesn't mean your competitors have to know about it!

You Are The Only Swimmer In The Pool!

Here is another approach, which can take some of the stress out of racing, as well as increase the standard of your performance. When you are about to swim a race, remind yourself that you have no one to compete with but yourself. Remind yourself that there is only one lane in the pool - yours, and you are the only swimmer on the block. Remind yourself that there are no other swimmers to worry about or be intimidated by, because every race is just like a time-trial, and you are the only one in the pool.

With the occasional exception, this is how you need to think to get your best results. Practice this in training, and in your meets. By taking the focus off the *obstacles* (your competition) you are then focusing upon your *goal,* and this is what you want to get the best out of

Mind Training for Swimmers

yourself. Your mind must always focus upon goals, not obstacles, in order to bring you your best performances in the pool.

This attitude also takes the pressure off yourself and frees up vital nervous energy, which you can use for your swim. Never look around at others during a race, and do not wonder if someone is coming up behind you. How can this possibly happen, anyway, because you are the only one in the pool, remember?

Pretend to yourself that the noise and splashing going on in the rest of the lanes is simply the sound of waves you are causing from the amazing power of your strokes. It certainly can't be coming from your competitors, because there is no one else in the pool, right? This can also reinforce to your mind how powerfully you are swimming.

You see, *mentally* it's possible to get your mind to believe almost *anything* if you can use your imagination well enough! You simply pretend to yourself that all conditions favour you perfectly, and nothing can go wrong. These are mental tricks you can play on your subconscious to extract a better time from your mind and body. I will talk more on this later under the subject of "role-playing".

When I mentioned that there are occasional exceptions, I mean that there are some super-competitive swimmers who actually thrive upon competing directly with their competitors, and they use this nervous energy they generate from this to fuel their swim. If this describes you, then go for it – whatever approach works for you is the one to use!

Mind Training for Swimmers

The Pessimism Method!

All swimmers are different, and believe it or not, some swimmers actually use the unusual approach of *pessimism* to take the pressure off!

Theis is not a 'mainstream' method and so it does not work for everyone - however as everyone is different, they are worth mentioning, in case they may be of help to you.

The Pessimism methods are where you mentally talk to yourself and tell yourself that you probably *won't* win the race (which is the complete opposite of what most people do). This approach allows some swimmers to go out to a race and swim *relaxed,* because they feel that there is *nothing expected of them.*

Remember that this will ONLY work for particular swimmers - do not use this method if you feel it pulls your confidence down! This is one of the negative side effects of this method if it does not suit you.

This method can be helpful for some swimmers who feel the pressure, but it will not work at all for others, so experiment to find out if this method is for you, as this is very important.

Here is your summary for this chapter, which does not contain any compulsory mental exercises for your Mental Training Program.

Summary

- When you feel the pressure of being *expected to win*, ask yourself some questions to find out just how important

Mind Training for Swimmers

the race really is - and this will lessen your anxiety; eg,
"Will the human race continue if I don't win this race?"

- Remember that you are always the only swimmer in the pool.

- Mentally pretend that the conditions are always perfect for you and nothing can possibly go wrong.

- If the pressure is getting to you at a meet, go outside and just watch the world go by for a short while, remembering that life will go on *regardless* of what happens in the pool.

- Ignore reputations of other swimmers, they mean nothing on the particular day you are swimming against them!

- Take some time out and divert your attention onto something else if you feel you are trying too hard - sometimes the harder we try, the worse things can get if we become too emotionally attached to our goal (remember how 'the zone' works?).

- If you begin stressing out at a meet, begin watching for 'uncontrollables' and cancelling them out, or refocusing your thoughts onto something else. Keep affirmations in mind as well, they are very handy during these times.

Mind Training for Swimmers

CHAPTER 12

Body Language - To Be A Champion Begin Acting Like One!

Champion swimmers behave differently to normal swimmers. They think differently, act differently, and swim differently. Not all the time of course, and not to create a lot of attention, but they all possess a special type of powerful body-language that lets their competitors know that they're a force to be reckoned with.

Of course, this is NOT saying they go around telling everyone how good they are - quite the opposite (as they certainly don't need to!) - instead they use their *actions and body language* to trigger fear into their competitors, and this is far more effective! To be a champion, you have to act like one, both in and out of the pool. This signals to both *yourself* and your *competitors* that you are mentally tough, successful and confident, like all champions are.

It has been shown that if you act in a particular way for long enough, it will eventually create new *neural connections* in your brain that will actually make that new behaviour a normal part of your personality. This means that if you act like a winner for long enough,

Mind Training for Swimmers

you will eventually *feel* like a winner - and if you continue to feel like a winner, you will eventually *become* a winner.

The best way to do this is to begin *acting like a winner* right now, through some subtle but powerful ways. It's silly to wait to *be* successful before you begin *acting* that way, because it might be a long wait! Better to begin feeling that way and getting used to it now, as it will increase your chances of future success in and out of the pool.

So what you do is this; think of a champion you particularly admire, and pick some of their mannerisms, behaviour and attitudes which you admire, and preferably ones you can easily identify with.

Then, you simply try each day to consciously bring these aspects into your own personality, keeping a mental picture of your champion in your mind as a reminder. Remember, *this does not mean* you should become egotistical or arrogant – quite the opposite, but it will increase your level of self-belief and confidence.

Also, it's useful to monitor the way you act around the pool before and after races at meets, because it is highly important to project a powerful image to all competitors at meets.

Here is a guideline:

- Imagine you are a champion when you are at the pool
- Behave like a successful swimmer would behave
- Speak the way a successful swimmer would speak
- Keep your head up, don't look down at the ground
- Stand and walk confidently

Mind Training for Swimmers

- Never say anything negative to other swimmers, always act positive
- Do not criticize or put other swimmers down – successful people never need to do this
- Always act as if the bad swims don't bother you at all, never show you are upset (at least, until you are away from your competitors' view!)
- Walk faster and more confidently when you feel down
- Exude (Only) Confidence To Your Competitors

Your competitors may often know nothing about you - and so all they have to go on is what they see. Meets are the time to put forward an image of power and confidence - not by being loud and obnoxious (!) but by projecting an image of a confident, powerful, relaxed swimmer (and NEVER allowing your competitors to see any sign of nerves or weakness).

As I mentioned before, winners are grinners, and so a smile to a friend is often a great sign of strength and confidence for your competitors to see! Keep your head up and act confident as though this race is just going to be a 'walk in the park'.

By acting this way, it will enhance your chances of success, because it's really difficult to act this way without beginning to *feel* that way as well! One of the most powerful methods of influencing your mind is through your body language, and meets are definitely the time to use this. This way you are not only putting a seed of doubt into your

Mind Training for Swimmers

competitors' minds, but also increasing your own level of confidence before the race.

Become "The Machine"

Remember my earlier reference to becoming known as 'the machine' - someone who remains positive *no matter what?* If you can maintain this attitude, eventually word will get around that you swim like an unstoppable, unbeatable machine, and that will really put some fear into their minds! Remember The Terminator in the old Arnold Schwartzenegger movies. No one wants to swim against a machine.

Here is your summary for this chapter, which does not contain any compulsory mental exercises for your Mental Training Program.

Summary

- Copy successful swimmers' habits, and begin to *act* the way a champion who you admire would act.
- Do not allow your competitors to see any sign of nerves whatsoever, but exude confidence and strength before races - this may be the only impression they may ever have of you!
- Become 'The Machine'!

CHAPTER 13

Increase Your Self-Awareness To Reach Greater Heights

The more you know about yourself, the more formidable you will be in the pool. "Knowing thyself" is one of the most potent weapons you can possess - because you more you know about yourself and the way your own mental and physical system works, the more you will be able to *extract* from yourself under the pressure of big races.

One of the best ways to increase your self-awareness is through compiling *lists*, which will slowly but surely create a revealing profile of yourself - which will give you all the information you need to swim at your best.

So this chapter is all about how jotting things down on paper can make a big difference to your performance in the pool. On top of the major benefits this information will provide, the very act of *writing* it can be very therapeutic. This can help to imprint positive information into your subconscious, plus help to relieve your mind of stress that will increase your mental and physical energy.

Mind Training for Swimmers

This chapter is generally filled with techniques that should be put into your mental training exercise book - unless I particularly specify otherwise. Here are a few things which have made a big difference to some swimmers I've worked with, and which you might consider putting into this book.

A Personal Success List

A winning streak, or momentum, is invaluable in any sport, but especially swimming. Yet when most swimmers achieve a goal, they immediately move on to the next goal, *forgetting all about what they had just achieved.* They totally waste the valuable use of its *energy, which* can create extra momentum for even better performances in future.

A Personal Success List makes maximum use of all past victories, and can help to provide you this extra momentum for better future performances. It usually helps to boost confidence substantially (and actually, I've never met a swimmer who didn't need a boost of confidence).

Put this list in your exercise book to take to meets, and it is also worthwhile to make another copy of this to hang up at home, as well. Here's how you create your Success List:

Make a list of all your *greatest swimming achievements*, writing down as many as you can think of (a minimum of 5). Some of your achievements may not even be races (eg. it may be a newspaper article which was written about you, or a compliment from a coach, former

Mind Training for Swimmers

champion etc). Anything that made you feel great about yourself and your swimming should go down on the list. It doesn't matter when, or how long ago it happened, put it down on the list anyway.

Make another copy of this list and place it somewhere it can be seen easily, such as beside your bed, or on the wall. You could even type it up nicely on computer and make it a feature (some people even frame it!).

Revue this list once a week, going over each item for 30 seconds, and allow your mind to *remember everything* that happened that day - how you *felt* emotionally after each race, and *re-create the excitement* of that victory all over again. This will allow you to use the energy of these past victories to send you on to even greater ones.

Constantly add to this list as you create even better performances over the year ahead, and when the list begins to get too long, take a few of the less-important ones off. Revue this list at least once during the week before any major meet.

This list reminds you how good you truly are, and creates the *feeling that you are a huge achiever.* This suggests to your mind that there is no reason why you shouldn't perform well this weekend as well. Some great times to refer to this list include:

- Before each important meet
- Every time you are feeling low in confidence, as it's a powerful way of bringing back confidence and positive attitude.

Mind Training for Swimmers

Remind yourself that you are *still* that very same person, only with more experience and a more advanced swimming technique. Here is an example of a Personal Success List.

PERSONAL SUCCESS LIST EXAMPLE
June 2005

- Swam a PB in Metropolitan - April '05
- Made State team 2003
- Won school meet Dec. '04
- Presented trophy in school assembly - Dec. '03
- Article in local newspaper - July '02
- (Michael Phelps / Ian Thorpe etc) told me I was swimming well – Nov. 2004

This Success List is a mandatory part of your mental training program, so do not overlook its importance!   Now, here is yet another way you can use lists to enhance your performance.

Try Creating A Rescue Plan

Every swimmer can go through times at a meet when they feel their confidence has disappeared - and something that can be very helpful when this happens (apart from your success list) is also a rescue plan.

Mind Training for Swimmers

A rescue plan is where you write down the aspects that you like the most about both *yourself, and your swimming* - to remind yourself of all the things that you have temporarily forgotten.

This rescue plan should be placed in your exercise book with your Success List and other information, and kept in your bag which you take with you to meets – as there is no point in leaving it at home when you need it most at the pool.

Find a fresh page and list down as many things as you can think of which you *honestly and truly like* about yourself and your swimming, and very briefly jot down *why* these things are so good. These aspects might be your strokes, your dives, your turns, your attitude, a particular stroke, or the fact that you are so strong in a particular event. It might be all of these and more!

While you're compiling this list, this is NOT a time to be modest! Write down every reason why you are absolutely fabulous, and don't hold back. No-one needs to ever see this list but you, so be totally honest with yourself and write these things down - because these are the *very things* which can pull you out of a 'down' patch if you need it in an emergency!

This is your rescue plan, which you can use (in conjunction with your success list) whenever you find that your confidence deserts you at a time when you need it most. By reminding yourself of your strengths, you are taking your mind off your weaknesses, which usually happens to be exactly what your mind is focusing upon whenever you lose your confidence.

Mind Training for Swimmers

Even the best swimmers go through times when they lose some faith in themselves - so be prepared in case it happens to you, have all the ammunition ready in case you need to rejuvenate your confidence.

Use A Journal To Overcome Problems

<u>Note</u>: Before I begin to describe how to use a journal, I recommend you do NOT put this journal in the exercise book you take along to meets, as it may contain some highly confidential and personal information, which you definitely want hidden away, not to be divulged to anyone who may find it in your bag at a meet.

I recommend you use a *separate* exercise book for this - as you want plenty of pages ready in case you need them, as you definitely don't want to lose concentration halfway through this exercise by searching for more paper. Now, let me show you how this works:

A normal part of competitive swimming is made up of dealing with problems that arise from time to time. If problems didn't arise, swimming would be extremely easy - but the fact is, swimming is always going to throw new challenges at you along the journey to success.

Most of the time a good way to deal with these problems is to verbalise them – that is, speak to someone about them, such as your coach, friend, parent, or a good listener, or someone who may be able to come up with some ideas to help. However, there are often some tender issues which everyone has a little trouble confiding in with others - and

Mind Training for Swimmers

this is why a journal can be invaluable when there is no one with whom to talk.

A journal is much like a diary, and you use it in a similar way to help your mind *process what is happening in your life at that particular time.* Simply by writing down *how you feel* about your swimming (and the challenges you are facing at that time) helps your mind process this information more clearly, and often surprisingly, even coming up with the perfect *answer.*

There is a very definite process required in using this method. The first thing you need is a blank page in your *separate* exercise book, where you can keep your journal. (Needless to say, keep this hidden away when you are not using it, as it may eventually contain information which you may not want read by anyone who happens to be walking into your room!). For this reason also, do not take your journal to meets, as this exercise is designed purely for use at home.

Before I go further, there *is* an exception to this rule. A few swimmers discovered that after races (especially *bad* races) jotting down some thoughts in their journal had been very helpful - especially at meets when none of their friends or family was able to attend. Their journal provided them with 'someone to talk to', and helped them to clarify their thoughts.

So if you feel that this may be helpful to you in this way, then by all means try it - but this is a decision for you to make. Or possibly you might take a fresh piece of paper to the pool to write on, rather than take

Mind Training for Swimmers

your journal with you - and you can staple the new notes into your journal when you get home.

Probably the most effective use of a journal is to write in it regularly, such as daily, or every 2-3 days, or otherwise every week. By doing this on a regular basis, you get better and more effective at using this technique. However, there is absolutely nothing wrong with purely using a journal for those particular times whenever you are feeling troubled about something, but when you have no-one to confide in about it at the time, to 'let off steam'.

All you do is begin writing about whatever issues are currently occurring in both your life and your swimming, almost as if you were writing a letter to a really close friend, who you can confide in. Don't hold anything back, write down what you *really feel* about these issues, such as your swimming, coaches, friends, your times, any fears you may have - everything that is important to you *at that time.*

No-one will ever read this but you - and you are the person who will benefit most out of reading it later, so don't hold any details back, put them all in there. It's very important to know that once you begin writing, *don't stop to read what you have written so far*, just keep writing until you cannot write any more - and you will instinctively know when this time is. This is a very important point - DO NOT STOP writing until you have finished!

Also, don't *think too hard* about what to write, just *write the first things that pop into your head* about the subject - this way you will record your true feelings, which is the whole point of the exercise.

Mind Training for Swimmers

If you ever have trouble beginning this exercise, simply start off by writing about the training you have done recently, and the meet you are preparing for, and then begin to add your *feelings* about these, plus any problems you might be experiencing. Once again, don't hold back - write exactly what you feel, as this is very important to get the full benefit out of this exercise.

Once you get the hang of it, there may be times where you might actually find it difficult to *stop* writing! When this happens, you are virtually writing directly from the subconscious mind – almost as if you are downloading the issue directly from your mind onto paper. And this is a great way to mentally *release* the problem - and surprisingly often, the problem may magically dissolve days or weeks after writing about it.

Once you have finished writing (and this might take just a few minutes or it could take 30 minutes, depending on how much you have to say) go back to the beginning and read the whole piece through from the beginning, as if it was something you were reading for the first time.

You may be very surprised to find that some of what you have written is *not* what you expected at all! What you have written is a *true record* of what you are feeling at that time, and this will help you to *understand yourself and your situation* much clearer, and often help you to find the solutions you need.

This is an invaluable exercise, so don't "write it off" - this can honestly help you to feel mentally stronger, more confident and positive about yourself and your swimming.

Mind Training for Swimmers

As I mentioned before, keeping a journal can also have the fabulous effect of *releasing pent-up frustration that* may have been holding you back. It is said that when Abraham Lincoln's desk was cleared out after he died, they found many letters he had written (to other heads of state, presidents etc) which vented his full anger, criticism and frustration – which seemed very odd as he did not seem to be the kind of person who would write such letters.

However, he had used these letters purely to vent his feelings, but (quite intelligently) he *never posted them!* He simply used them to help himself overcome the frustrations he felt inside, so he could move forward positively. And you can do the same.

In fact, I have worked with several swimmers over the years who had *so* much anger and rage inside them that I asked them to do something a little different – I asked them to write about their issue in a journal, then read it, and then last of all, *burn it!* I told them to burn the pages for two reasons – one was to ensure that the information remained private and never got into the wrong hands, and secondly, burning the pages almost became a ceremonial, symbolic gesture to show that the issue was now *gone forever.* The swimmers who did this said that this helped them a great deal with both the issue, and also their anger about it.

A good time to write in your journal is at night, as this helps your mind go over the day's happenings and process them properly before you go to sleep. As I said, this is purely a private journal, so keep your innermost thoughts hidden away from prying eyes, as you may not want

Mind Training for Swimmers

others to read them (especially if you've written something *negative* about someone, which you may have only felt at the particular time you wrote it!).

So consider beginning a journal, and you may well notice the difference in your attitude, especially *to the things that used to bother you.* You may notice a big difference in your ability to handle pressure, which never goes astray for a competitive swimmer!

PS. One last time - remember, it's generally recommended you do <u>not</u> put this journal in the exercise book you take along to meets (unless you decide otherwise), as it may contain personal information you do not wish to be accidentally seen by others.

An Exercise in Belief....

If you have trouble overcoming a particular mental hurdle, such as breaking a certain time, or not being able to beat a particular competitor, then this means that your mind knows *more reasons why you can't do it*, than reasons why you *can.*

A way of moving beyond this problem can be to create a 'List Of Reasons Why You WILL Achieve Your Goal'. This can help to overturn a particularly strong negative belief, and create positive new performances. This is how to do it:

Find a blank page in your exercise book and number down the left hand side of each line, continuing over several pages until you have numbered 200 lines. Put a heading at the top "Reasons why I WILL achieve my Goal".

Mind Training for Swimmers

Then, every day or two, write down the first 3 or more reasons *that come to mind* as to why you CAN achieve your goal. It doesn't matter if some of these are a repeat of past reasons you have listed, just write them down anyway, and if you can think of more, then keep writing. An important part of this is that after writing down your reasons for each particular day, finish by *reading through the whole list* that you have compiled so far. This cements into your mind the reasons why you will be able to achieve what you want.

Eventually, after the passing of weeks, or possibly even months, you will have written down 200 reasons why you will achieve your goal. By this time you will find that your belief regarding this issue should have somewhat changed - in some cases completely. This is because by the end of this exercise your mind will know *more reasons why you can achieve your goal, than reasons why you can't.* Once you reach this point, achieving the goal becomes much easier, because your mind will be working *with* you, instead of against you. Here is an example below of a Reasons List.

<u>Reasons Why I WILL Achieve My Goal</u>

- My times are coming down in training.
- I am fitter than I have been for a long time.
- My coach thinks I can still improve a lot.
- My diet is getting better.
- I am doing mental training & others aren't.

Mind Training for Swimmers

- (Aaron Peirsol / Natalie Coughlin / Grant Hackett etc) once told me I had a great style.
- I'm training well.
- I know I am still improving.
- I'm concentrating now on my main events.
- I've always been a good at long distances.
- Etc.

Here is your summary for this chapter, containing one compulsory mental exercise for your Mental Training Program.

Summary

- Mental Training Program:
  Create a personal success List and revue it regularly, especially in the week before an important meet. Using this regularly will dramatically boost your confidence.
- Keep a personal journal to help your mind process problems and come up with new solutions. Keep this in a separate book to the other lists.
- Create a rescue plan for times when you may need it, by listing all your strengths about yourself and your swimming - and make sure you USE it when you most need it!
- If your belief is failing, it could be you need more positive reasons for your mind to focus upon - so try the

Mind Training for Swimmers

Reasons List to help increase belief. PS. Don't forget the mirror technique as well.

- Put your mood chart and list of goals in your exercise book as well.

CHAPTER 14

Overcoming Slumps In Form & The Power of Role-Playing

Everyone goes through slumps in form at some stage in their career - or even just a time where you may not have done a PB for a while. These periods are not anything to particularly worry about, as everyone goes through them, even the champions. In fact, it almost seems that in order to reach the highest levels, a swimmer must go through this 'test' at certain periods in their career - so once again, it is nothing to worry about.

These are simply times, which test your persistence and determination, qualities common in all champions - who are often renowned for coming back from 'nowhere' to make a successful swim.

However, this may still be a good time to make use of your Success List and also your journal. The Success List will help to bring the confidence levels back up, and the journal will help to release any pent-up emotion and stress that you may have been storing (and may have been holding you back). Also, needless to say, daily visualization

Mind Training for Swimmers

and affirmations are a *must* during times when you are feeling down about your swimming.

It's important to know that slumps in form can also be an *opportunity* - because they can be a signal for you to make some changes to your routine and possibly try a new approach, which often results in greater improvement.

This is why two of the most important qualities during slumps are persistence and experimentation. Persistence is what you need to help you get through the difficult times, and experimentation often discovers the solution to the problem. Experimentation means to bring some *change* into your routine. Talk to your coach and ask if there are any changes which may help you get through this period - such as changes in your stroke, your sets or your other training. Needless to say, communication with your coach during times like this is highly important - find out what they think and any suggestions they may have.

Often change alone can break a swimmer out of a rut - many swimmers can become too familiar and bored with the same routines if starved of variety in their training for too long.

The bottom line, however, is that you must always realize that 'dry spells' are just *temporary phases*, it's just a matter of believing in yourself, persisting, and using some experimentation in order to get things moving again. Never doubt your ability to turn things around, hang in there because great performances could be just around the corner.

Mind Training for Swimmers

Role-Play - To Bring Out Your Best On The Day

Some swimmers perform better when the pressure is off; while some perform better when it's on. It's important to find out which of these types you are, because this information can bring out your best in the big meets. So which one are you? Think about this now before we go any further.

OK, now that you have an idea about which type you are (if not, pause here and think about it!), let's discuss a handy tool called *role-playing*, which is a trick you play on your mind to get more out of your swim. There is almost no limit to the range of possibilities in this technique - your imagination can come up with a limitless range - just ensure that they are always positive. Here are some examples of role-playing and how it works.

Let's say you've decided that you perform better with *less* pressure. You could then role-play by imagining to yourself that you'll be competing against the hottest State, National or world ranked swimmers, who are being predicted to blow you out of the water! This means that you can mentally relax - as "no-one expects me to win", and this allows you to swim *without any pressure of expectation.* Ironically, this will often bring out your best performance!

You simply keep running this scenario through your mind before the race, imagining that no one expects you to win and that you are the underdog. This can also often trigger a burst of energy and motivation in your bid to *prove them all wrong.* This is one of many approaches to take some pressure off of you.

Mind Training for Swimmers

Now here is a totally opposite approach. This approach applies if you have decided you perform *better* when the pressure of expectation is upon you, and you are expected to do well.

This is where you imagine the exact opposite scenario. You would imagine that you are by far the *best* swimmer in the race, and that *all eyes are upon you* to see what time you are going to do - because it's almost *expected* that you will win.

This approach gets the competitive juices flowing (for this particular type of swimmer), and builds motivation for the race - and works especially well if you feel unmotivated because *others* do not expect you to win.

In this case, you would visualize having all the attention upon you (yes, even if it isn't) and that your competitors are highly intimidated by having you in their race.

This approach works well for those who thrive under the bright glare of attention, and perform better when the pressure is on. This is quite common in some swimmers, who thrive on being star performers - and this is the way to rev yourself up if you are the type of swimmer that is motivated in this way.

Of course, it's essential to know which type of swimmer you are before you can do this - most swimmers tend to be definitely one type or another, so begin to notice whether you *like* attention, or avoid it.

This will give you a clue as to the best way to motivate yourself, using mind games such as these. In a way, this technique is much like

Mind Training for Swimmers

visualization - simply running a movie or scenario through your mind that you want your mind to accept as true.

Bend Your Reality

Role-playing can be done in almost any way you require, at any given time. For instance, if you feel the pool is a slow pool, pretend to yourself that it's fast, and use all your imagination to ensure that you convince your subconscious mind that this is so. Or if you feel your competitors are catching up on you, pretend that instead you are moving further ahead.

The key is to bend your reality to suit your circumstances, because humans have the ability to do this quite easily with their powerful imaginations. The more creative your imagination, the easier you will find this to do!

This can work remarkably well in almost any situation, as now you can turn *almost any circumstance around to suit you perfectly*, simply by bending the facts a little in your mind - instead of feeling at a disadvantage. Try it and see if it makes a difference. So begin experimenting with this technique and see if it brings 'that little extra' out of your performance.

Here is your summary for this chapter, which does not contain any compulsory mental exercises for your Mental Training Program.

Mind Training for Swimmers

Summary

- If your confidence levels change from day to day, do not worry too much as this is completely normal - however if it is swinging wildly from highs to lows, use daily visualizations and affirmations to boost it up. Remember your Success List and Journal can also help.

- Sometimes slumps are in fact an opportunity designed to challenge you further, and bring out your very best.

- If you ever go through a slow patch of improvement, use *persistence and experimentation* to move through it - and discuss some changes with your coach.

- Make the conditions *perfect* for yourself every time by role-playing scenarios in your mind at meets. Find out what type of swimmer you are - do you perform better or worse under pressure? Role-play to discover whether you need to take the pressure off, or rev yourself up.

CHAPTER 15

Some Important Notes

This chapter covers a wide range of different subjects, which often arise in swimming - demonstrating various techniques and how to overcome problems that commonly arise. Whilst most of the topics will apply to you, there may be some topics that are *less* relevant to you at the current time, so when this happens simply move on to the next topic listed.

A Formula For Success

Your mental training must become not only a *daily habit,* but become a powerful *routine* where you have a method that delivers consistently successful results for you at the meets. At the same time, it should also be able to help you overcome any problems that may arise along the way, such as nerves, intimidation, excessive worrying, etc.

So what I am really saying is that you must develop your own mental and physical *formula for success.* Every champion swimmer has developed specific mental and physical routines that help them achieve their goals at the meets. These routines do not mean that they are able to

Mind Training for Swimmers

win every single race, but they do ensure they achieve a high level of overall success.

This is one of the great secrets of success – creating a successful formula which produces consistently strong results, and which fits comfortably with your own personality and lifestyle.

Success lies in your routines – all of them, not only your daily routine, but also your pre-meet routines, and not just your physical routines, but also your *mental* routines. So experiment with these and monitor your results - the quickest way to find it is to jot down which methods *work* for you, and which do not – and slowly but surely you begin to create your own personal 'formula for success'.

Once you have established a successful formula, there may never again be a need to deviate from it, as long as it continues to deliver successful results for you. Remember, once you have mastered your mind, you will have mastered your body as well.

You Must Learn To Bounce Back!

One of the toughest times in swimming is when you physically and mentally prepare yourself for a big meet, only to find that you fail to achieve your goal. Or even worse, having a meet where you don't even come *close*).

When this happens (and it happens to everyone) the first thing to do is to realise that EVERY swimmer goes through this. Not just some swimmers - every single swimmer. Defeat is not something new, and you did not invent it! Even the most successful swimmers go through

Mind Training for Swimmers

this, and they are the ones who have learned the powerful art of *bouncing back* from the jaws of defeat, to achieve ultimate victory. More on this in a moment.

Secondly, it's not the unsuccessful meet, which will have an affect upon your future success, but your REACTION to that meet which is most important. This means you must not dwell negatively upon the meet, but extract whatever positives you can possibly discover from it, LEARN from the experience, and then, most importantly, MOVE ON to new goals.

The trap lies in dwelling upon the past. Instead you must move forward, and focus upon greater triumphs to come. This is the key to success, and I call this 'bouncing back' - the quality of all great champions.

Of course, there's no point moving forward blindly. You must find out what you need to know from those swims, and then arm yourself with this information to return *better, faster, hungrier* and *more powerful* than before. Successful swimmers bounce back from failures, and convert them into future victories.

So don't fall into the self-pity trap or mentally torture yourself after a bad race, like most swimmers do – instead, get on with it and DO something about it. Talk to your coach, examine what went wrong, plan a new strategy - and then move forward positively. This will ensure that you will have your day. Use setbacks to make yourself stronger, and eventually you will be indestructible. Once again - use setbacks to make yourself even stronger!!

Mind Training for Swimmers

When a great swimmer "fails", this can actually strike FEAR into their competitors - who usually know (only too well) that this particular swimmer will only come back again - faster, harder and stronger than before. This is what the greatest athletes do, they convert failures into future victories. They use these "failures" to gather even more mental and physical 'ammunition' to return even stronger the next time. So learn to bounce back - it's one of the most powerful qualities you can ever possess.

The Excuse Trap

One of the biggest and easiest traps to fall into right before a big race or event is to allow your mind to create excuses for you. This is a very common trap, where your mind basically gives you *permission* to swim a mediocre race – and this does not bring great performances. For instance, you might find yourself thinking something like: "I was sick a few weeks ago, so if I don't swim well, that will be why". Or maybe something like "my coach tapered my training incorrectly, and so if I lose badly, THAT will be to blame, not me".

These sorts of thoughts are generally the kiss of death to your chances of swimming well, and should usually be avoided at all times. Once your mind focuses upon a reason why you may *not* swim well, it then programs your body's performance along the lines of "you have permission to swim badly". Most often this type of thinking creates a sub-standard performance. Remember, your mind is the computer which

Mind Training for Swimmers

programs your body's swim, and so the thoughts you are thinking before a race are the data which is basically *programming* your result.

Finding someone to blame (in advance) is a classic negative thought before a race. You often hear all the gripes after a race is over, such as how *everyone else* is to blame – everyone except himself or herself. This attitude basically gets a swimmer *no-where fast*.

Some swimmers even use excuses to attempt to *psych out* their competitors. Often they will offer their competitors an excuse right before a race, which is designed to reduce the pressure upon themselves - and increase the pressure on their competitors!

Unfortunately this negative tactic can occasionally work in their favour - but the good news is that, in general, excuses simply create bad results. The bottom line is that "excuse merchants" generally do NOT become champion swimmers.

Every swimmer however, is different – and there will always be a few exceptions to the rule. I've found that around 5% of swimmers actually *do* swim better when they reduce the pressure upon themselves by using negative excuses such as these.

Australian Olympic gold medallist Susie O'Neill used the *quietly negative approach* for many years with great success - but she was highly unusual in this way. You rarely (if ever) hear the likes of Michael Phelps, Ian Thorpe, Inge DeBruijn, Grant Hackett, Lenny Krazelburg or Gary Hall Jr giving excuses before a race. They keep their focus quietly positive and upbeat at all times.

Mind Training for Swimmers

Remember that if around 5% of swimmers *benefit* from excuses, this means that a whopping 95% of swimmers are much better off focusing upon positive thoughts. Positive thoughts bring positive results, and negative thoughts bring negative results, always keep this age-old truth in mind. You will usually get what you EXPECT - so make sure you expect the best!

Watch out for These Traps

When you are at a meet, there are all kinds of silent hazards to beware, which can affect your mental attitude (and your races). Worst of all, many swimmers don't even know *they are there*. Recognizing these hazards is the main step towards creating a successful mindset, as many swimmers don't recognise these negatives, and simply allow their mental approach (and their races) to be silently sabotaged - without even knowing it.

I will go into some of these hazards in a moment, but first, let me explain the most effective way to remain positive before races. The best way to remain focused and positive at a meet is to regularly "check in" on your thoughts every 10 or 20 minutes, to ensure that your thinking is remaining positively on track for a successful meet. This allows you to *notice the thoughts you are thinking* each time you check in, and eradicate any negative thoughts immediately the instant they begin to form – and before they grow more powerful. This is essential, as once these negative thoughts begin to take effect, they are very difficult to overcome.

Mind Training for Swimmers

It's also very important to keep a watchful eye out for other potential *saboteurs* which may be intent on bringing about your swimming destruction - let me show you what I mean. Here are just a few very powerful *silent saboteurs* to watch out for at meets.

- *Uncontrollables - the powerful negative thoughts that focus upon all the things you absolutely cannot control.*
  As we have mentioned before, these types of negative thoughts can range in the hundreds - such as the amount of swimmers in the warm-up pool, the temperature of the water, the lane you are swimming in, the size and physique of your competitors, etc etc. These thoughts create anxiety, which constrict the muscles and reduce the blood flow, thus reducing your performance in the pool. You must watch for these thoughts very closely at meets, and stop them immediately before they take effect.

- *Comparisons - mentally comparing yourself to your competitors, such as their physiques, performances or times.*
  Never, ever do this - unless you know that the comparison will bring you out on top. Comparisons generally focuses your mind upon your *shortcomings* rather than your assets, and this type of thinking needs to be immediately changed to focusing upon your *strengths*.

Mind Training for Swimmers

- *Competitors (or their coaches / friends or parents) who plant negative thoughts in your mind.*

  This can be very common and also extremely subtle, making it very difficult to detect. For instance, someone may ask you what your best time or performance is right before a race, followed by kindly informing you that they have done a much better time or performance. Or they may inform you about every single *great* swim they have ever swum in recent times. If you're not careful, this can unknowingly set off a string of negative thoughts before a race, which could eventually lead to a bad performance. (By the way, a *great* response to these comments is to say "wow, you should do really well in this race then!" This puts the pressure right back on *them)*. Others who use psychological warfare may use this *reverse* method to put pressure on you, by mentioning things such along such lines as "you have had such good results, you will do much better than me today". Of course, this *could* also be a truthful comment made to you by a friend, but always make sure you can spot the authentic ones from the fake ones!

These are just *some* of the saboteurs for which you must watch. You can only overcome the hurdles you *about which you are aware* - so always be aware of any influences upon your mental attitude whilst you

Mind Training for Swimmers

are at meets, especially before races. Do this by regularly 'checking in' on your thoughts, to eavesdrop on what your mind is thinking. Always remember that on many occasions, many races are often won *before they even start.*

The Secret Of Consistency

Are your results always strong and consistent, or do you experience extreme highs and lows, up and own like a yo-yo? It seems that some swimmers would do almost anything for more *consistency* in their results, which can sometimes range from absolutely brilliant, right through to terrible, all on the very same day.

So where can you buy some consistency? There's only one place you can get it, and of course, it's in your mind. Consistency in your body originates from consistency in your mind.

Let me say this again - if you want consistency from *your body*, you must have consistency in *your mind*. This means that if you put in a consistent daily effort in your training, you will achieve consistent, solid results in your meets.

This is not always easy. There will always be occasional training days when you will feel less inspired, less strong or less energised than you normally would - but the key is to put in the same amount of mental and physical energy anyway, *regardless of how you feel*. It is often said that the true secret to success comes from mental and physical consistency in your daily training.

Mind Training for Swimmers

Swimmers who put in strong training sessions one day, but *slack off* a little the next tend to be 'streaky' in their meet results - achieving some great results, but also some terrible ones. This generally is not what you want - and it can also cause uncertainty and stress before races.

When your mind and body reach a point where they *expect* to put in a strong performance (similar to the daily efforts you have put in at training for the past two or three years), that is generally what they will provide for you.

The key is to make your body *so machine-like in its daily performance* that it will provide you with a good time *even when you don't feel at your best.* I'm sure that you've heard that success lies in our daily habits, and this doesn't just mean swimming every day, but swimming *with a purpose* every day.

Of course, this is not to say that you should do try to do this if you are feeling ill - but assuming that you are feel physically OK, always try to put in a similar, consistent effort each day - both physically and mentally. Doing this *routines* your mind into *expecting* consistency from your results, and this will begin to be reflected in your results at the meets.

Basically what I am saying is to make consistency one of your *daily habits*, not something you hope will occur the day of a big meet. If you make consistency a natural way of life, then you will know what to expect when you go out to swim in a meet, instead of wondering what results your body is going to deliver for you that day!

Mind Training for Swimmers

They say success lies in our daily habits, and this is so true - your training is the key to your success, so use it wisely. Your attitude each day is going to reflect your results in the meets - so how is your attitude today? Are you ready to put in a strong, consistent effort?

Are You Getting The Most Out Of Your Coach?

To be successful it is important to *make the most* out of every single area involved in your swimming. One of these essential areas is your coach, who is your partner along your journey to success.

So an important question is this; is your coach approachable, and do you communicate well with them? Or do you turn up for training, do your sets and leave without as much as saying a word to him or her?

It's essential that you be able to communicate freely with your coach so that you can let them know how you're feeling about your swimming (especially when you're feeling down) and equally important that you know how your coach *feels about your progress.*

There may be times when another direction needs to be taken with your plan of attack, and these are things that need to be discussed sooner rather than later. The ability of your coach to communicate with you is highly important, and should not be underestimated. If this area is not satisfactory, it's essential to try and improve the situation - or if this does not seem to help, consider changing your coach.

Another aspect worth checking is your progress - do you feel satisfied with your rate of improvement, or do you feel that you've not been making the most of your ability? If the latter is the case, then

Mind Training for Swimmers

communicating this to your coach is essential. Let them know how you feel and ask their opinion as to how they think you can change this situation.

Also, the sets you do each day must be varied occasionally, as boredom is one of the greatest killers of motivation (in not only swimming, but any area of life). Check that you are not becoming bored with the same routines - if you are, ask for some new sets from your coach, or even suggest some yourself.

Once again, if your coach is not open to communication or new ideas, this is an area that must be addressed very quickly. Your coach is a major part of your future success, and it is essential that you are happy in this area, as success is very difficult without it.

Create An Inspirational Collage

A great little daily motivator at home is to create a motivational *collage* for your swimming. A collage, (pronounced 'coll-arge', with a soft 'g'), is a large piece of cardboard onto which you paste pictures of successful swimmers you admire, inspirational quotes that give you a lift – basically anything that makes you think of *successful swimming.*

You pin your collage onto a wall in your bedroom, somewhere that you will regularly see it each day - and your subconscious mind will mentally 'scan' it each time you walk by (whether you consciously realise it or not). I've even heard of some swimmers even putting their collages on the ceiling above their bed, so they'll wake up to it every morning!

Mind Training for Swimmers

A collage can be used as a powerful ally, or a source of inspiration before meets, especially during times when you need a boost of confidence or motivation. It doesn't matter what you put on the collage as long as it inspires you - that is its sole purpose. Quotes, newspaper articles, photos, thoughts.....anything that is visually motivating to you.

Whenever you see an article or photo in the newspaper or a magazine that inspires you, cut it out and add it to your collage. Eventually it will become a fabulous colourful feature of your bedroom wall, and also a powerful tool to inspire you!

You may even like to paste your 'Success List' onto it as well - so that you are up there with the other champions. I've known some swimmers to even paste photos of their own heads onto photos of their favourite Olympian's body, so that they have a picture of themselves holding a gold medal! A collage is a powerful way of both consciously *and* subconsciously working on your mental training – give it some thought.

Don't Obsess About Your Competitors

One of the most important points, but often the most forgotten, is to focus on the goal and not the obstacles. Your competitors definitely appear under the category of obstacles - which means the more you focus upon them, the more they will affect you. Never worry or obsess about against who you will be swimming.. Instead, let them worry about you!

Mind Training for Swimmers

This is not always easy of course, but I have now taught you several ways to focus your mind onto the positive, such as 'cancelling' out the negative thoughts, and re-focusing your mind back onto your goal. Focusing upon your own swim is highly important because, as I've mentioned before, generally the best races you will ever swim will be when you can completely focus upon your *own* lane, and not anyone else's. Leave it to your competitors to worry about you!

If You Want Success...

Believe it or not, another essential quality for success is happiness – as true success is very difficult without it. To be able to attain the results you want, you often need to work harder than most people would like - and this is only possible (in the long-term) if you truly love what you are doing.

This is not to say that you have to *love* every moment of your swimming (such as getting up early every morning, the winter mornings, etc), but overall you must enjoy what you are doing or you will find that, as time goes by, you will become less inclined to put in the extra effort required to be successful.

This is why swimmers who are being driven towards success by *others* - such as parents or coaches, are invariably the swimmers who drop out forever and never swim another stroke. Motivation must come from *within* if you really want to succeed - not from other people. All champions are self-motivated people. Sure they have their coaches and

Mind Training for Swimmers

other people encouraging them, but the true motivation comes from within.

So do a 'happiness check' often - and if you find you are becoming disillusioned, find out why, immediately - and fix it. This is essential if you wish to remain devoted to the sport.

Many of us can manage to drive ourselves to achieve things we don't like - but not usually for much longer than a couple of years, and it usually takes longer than this, of course, to attain real success in swimming.

It's interesting to notice that generally the best opportunities always seem to go to those who approach the meets as a *fun challenge*, rather than as an *ordeal*. Opportunities just seem to naturally flow to those who are enjoying what they do - and these are the people who end up in the Success Club.

Happiness is an important ingredient to our motivation, so if you want to be there for the long-term success, make sure you're having a good time!

If There's A Crowd, Use Their Energy!

A big crowd at a meet can often make or break a swimmer, though many swimmers quite often ignore this factor. This occurs because every swimmer (consciously or unconsciously) either *uses the crowd* to drive them to greater heights, or *allows them* to negatively affect their performance.

Mind Training for Swimmers

Of course, it can also depend a little on whether the crowd is going for you or not! But here is where you can use some of your mental training expertise. Even if the crowd are cheering for another swimmer, you can easily alter your perception, and imagine in your mind that the crowd are cheering *you!* This is part of the role-playing method I spoke about previously.

If a crowd helps to inspire you to better times, *use them*, it doesn't matter whether they are calling your name or not! If they are cheering one of your competitors, simply bend your reality a little, and imagine that every single person at the pool is calling out *your* name.

Seeing the crowd have made the effort to turn up, you may as well put them to good use. Remember that mentally tough swimmers are *opportunists*, and are always ready to accept any little advantage which is (legally) made available to them - and so if this means accepting the crowd's support, so be it!

On the other hand, if you are a swimmer who is badly affected by crowds (and there are lots of swimmers out there in this category), using the 'curtain visualization' I mentioned earlier can help.

This is where you imagine that you are swimming in a lane that is cloaked by black curtains on each side of your lane, so no one can see you swimming your race. This works really well and helps take the pressure off.

Always remember that it's the *tiny things that make a huge difference* – especially in a sport such as swimming.

Mind Training for Swimmers

Be Mentally Fresh For Meets

If you feel you are thinking or obsessing too much about an approaching meet, get away from your normal routine and do something a little different. Go to a movie or visit a friend, just to get your mind off the meet for a while. You *do not want every waking thought to be about swimming*, or you will waste your mental energy before the meet.

Here is your summary for this chapter, which does not contain any compulsory mental exercises for your Mental Training Program.

Summary

- Regularly check that you are generally happy with your swimming, as it's an essential ingredient for success. If something is blocking your enjoyment, fix it immediately, or it may affect your motivation, vital to your long-term success.
- Begin creating your own personal formula for success, by noting all the aspects, physically and mentally, which work for you - and discontinuing those aspects that do not.
- Create an inspirational collage to boost your motivation at home.
- Make sure the communication lines are open with your coach, and check to see if you are motivated by the training he or she provides. Otherwise, work on improving these aspects. If this does not happen, make

Mind Training for Swimmers

whatever changes necessary to ensure you are happy with your progress and motivation.

- Success becomes a mental and physical formula that champions adhere to – so begin noticing what does (and doesn't) work for you, and begin creating your own formula for success.

- To experience *consistency* in your meet results, you must put the same effort into your training. This *conditions* your mind and body to put in strong effort every time, rather than conditioning yourself for inconsistency.

- If you have a large crowd watching, use their energy by imagining that they are all cheering for you! Otherwise, if you prefer to have no crowds at all, you can use the 'black curtain' visualization method, to take the pressure off.

Mind Training for Swimmers

CHAPTER 16

The Last Word

Visualization - Use It And Maintain It

The most important thing about mental training is to DO it. However this can be a difficult thing to maintain at times, especially when we get busy, or if your daily visualization becomes overly familiar or a little boring.

This is why it is essential to occasionally inject variety into your visualizations, with different music, imagery, locations and competitors, and even different *perspectives* can help. For instance, if you visualize your swimming from a viewpoint *above your body* (looking down at yourself), then possibly you might like to try being *in your body* for a change. Or vice versa. Either of these methods works well, and you can also change from one to the other without any problem.

As you know, there are many different ways you can use visualization - to improve technique problems, intimidation, nervousness etc. For instance, some swimmers find that when they are working on *technique* in the visualizations, it often works better viewing the swim

Mind Training for Swimmers

from *inside* their body, rather than from above it – but if the other way works best for you, go for it. It can also help to visualize the swim in *slow motion* so that you can ensure that every technical aspect of your movements are perfect - before finishing with another normal-speed version of the swim. Others find it difficult to *create pictures* in their mind and find that they are better to simply *feel* the new stroking technique, rather than actually seeing it – and this also works fabulously well.

The thing to remember is that it doesn't matter what problems you experience - you can find solutions to virtually all of them using this technique. There is almost no physical problem that cannot be improved using mental training - it's just a matter of using this technique to its capacity each day.

Anything you choose to *work on* during your daily visualization will eventually show steady improvement - because you are giving it constant daily attention. This is they key.

For instance, if someone intimidates you, fix it. Go into your inner world each day, and *change* the situation until it eventually changes *for real*. This applies to anything that you feel could be holding you back - go to the *inner gym*, work on it and change it.

Think of visualization as a secret weapon which you can use to help you in all kinds of different ways – don't limit it to just improving your times, it can do so much more than this. The main thing is to find a time to DO the visualization, because as long as you can manage this,

Mind Training for Swimmers

you will remain amongst the small *minority* of swimmers who have this distinct advantage in the pool.

I say this because most *average* swimmers either don't use mental training, or don't know *how* to use it, or simply do not possess the willpower to keep it up - and this puts you at a distinct advantage *as long as you continue on your mental training program.*

At the elite level of course, there are few swimmers who don't have *some* kind of mental preparation. The funny thing is that some swimmers don't even *know* they are visualizing, they just do it naturally by projecting their mind forward to the race ahead. So some swimmers say they don't do any mental training, when in fact they actually do, they just don't know it!

If you can find a regular time in the day to visualize, this makes it much easier - but otherwise, just do it whenever you can. Whatever mental training you can do is probably something that your competitors *aren't* doing! So take your visualization seriously and make the effort to do it regularly - every day if you can.

If you miss a day here or there, don't let that stop you or reduce your motivation, just make sure you do it the next day. You want to make it a way of life, a daily habit like cleaning your teeth - so that it actually feels strange when you *don't* do it.

This way your mind gets into a steady *rhythm* with the mental training, and *expects* to do it each day, and eventually you may find that as soon as you close your eyes to visualize, your mind will automatically begin to click right into the visualization!

Mind Training for Swimmers

Creating this type of mental training routine makes the effect from the exercise much more powerful, and this is only brought about by making it a daily *habit*. Be determined to maintain this as your little "secret weapon", and it will always look after you in meets - almost like having your own guardian angel!

Swimmer Amnesia

Mental training is very rarely given credit for the vast improvements it creates in swimming and other sports. I don't know how many times I worked with swimmers who were in depths of despair about their swimming, only to find that some months later, after they had improved their performances immensely and achieved new personal best times, they had *completely forgotten* exactly what had brought about the positive changes!

Despite the fact that their physical training had remained *identical* to the time when things had been going badly for them, and that the mental training was the only new innovation they'd tried, they still scratched their heads as to why they were "suddenly swimming really well". Many seemed to put it down to some mystical stroking improvement they must have picked up somehow in the last 3 months!

This is how mental training works however – silently but effectively. It's the aspects that you *no longer notice* which is where mental training makes the biggest differences – for instance, major long-term problems such as extreme nervousness or intimidation by other swimmers can suddenly disappear. These aspects can go unnoticed by

Mind Training for Swimmers

the swimmer, who may often just think they've just had a "really good day in the pool". Some even seem to forget that they had even had a problem in the first place!

But actually, it's very important to know why you have improved, because it is a powerful reinforcement of your own personal power – of your own mind and body. Plus it will remind you to continue your mental training, purely and simply because it works.

Before Races – Read This Pre-Race Psych-Up

This is a pre-race psych-up article for you to read and inspire yourself before you swim – you may even want to record it and play it back to yourself before big races. Here goes:

There is no one like you. You are unique. There is no one to compete with, because you are different from the rest. No one has your strokes, technique, mind or body – no one but you. This is where you have the advantage. You are armed with the most powerful computer in the world - your mind, which runs your body to the exact instructions you give it. Others also have this, but you have a major advantage because you are one of the few people who knows *how to use it*!

You have the ability within you - right now - to swim the perfect race, and do it all effortlessly. Your body has the ability to create its own adrenaline, and power you along even faster than you have ever imagined. You have within your memory bank the know-how to swim the perfect race. Because every single race and lap you have every swum

Mind Training for Swimmers

in your life is recorded there, just waiting to be used once more – and all your best dives, strokes and turns are about to happen all in the one race.

There is virtually nothing you are not capable of when you put this amazing mechanism to work. You are a walking miracle, capable of unbelievable feats. Never doubt this, not even for a moment.

There is no point comparing yourself to others, because there is no one in this world exactly like you, and there never will be. The mould was broken once you were born to this world, and you are here to do things that no one else can do, quite the way you can. Everywhere you go, your total uniqueness follows you.

You are capable at any time of swimming better, faster and stronger than ever before. You have the ability within you to make the absolute most of your strokes, talent and mental strength. You can even overcome physical problems if required, because remember, it's your mind that controls your body.

Every day so-called 'miracles' are happening in sport, and the mind is the power behind them. You have this power also. You are powerful, unique and unlimited. There is nothing to stop you, because this power is available to you at all times. So why not use it now?

It's time you showed the world what you can really do. It's time to let them know what you really are capable of (and you may have been the only one who has really known, all this time). Allow the strength and the passion burning inside your heart to explode into the greatest performance you possess deep within you; the time is now to show yourself, and everyone else, who you really are.

Mind Training for Swimmers

So go out there and make it happen - don't think about it, just do it naturally. Every person has a time in their life, which turns their life around forever, and now is that time. Your time is now. So go out there and do it. There is nothing to stop you, and nothing can get in your way. GO FOR IT!

Revise This Book Regularly
To Avoid Falling Back Into Negative Ways

Humans learn things, put them into practice, but then, often forget about them again. This is why we can find ourselves sometimes falling back into the same old habits we used to fall into.

A classic example of this is maintaining a positive thought pattern - I find this is one area many people forget about. Many people start out on their "mental diet" and manage to successfully create a positive thought pattern - but then forget to continue to *monitor it*, and without knowing it, they begin to fall back into the negative thoughts again. It is essential you keep an eye out for this.

Whenever you feel that you are falling back into old habits, begin reviewing this book again, as well as the summaries and any notes you may have taken, and notice which subjects "ring bells" for you – and it will become fairly obvious to you what you need to work on to correct the problem.

For this reason, and to speed up the process, I had drafted out Your Mental Training Checklist in the last chapter, which is probably the best way of *quickly* noticing where you may need to focus your

Mind Training for Swimmers

attention. Review this every six months to check on the areas you may need to work on.

Comparing Yourself With Faster Swimmers – Good Or Bad?

One of the *worst* things for self-confidence, yet one of the *best* things for improvement, is to regularly *compare yourself to better swimmers* in your own team or squad. Yes - I know this doesn't seem to make sense, so let me explain.

A swimmer once asked me about whether it was good to compare yourself with other swimmers, and my answer was that it was a 'double-edged sword' – meaning that depending on your personality type, it can be either good *or* bad for you.

Swimmers who may be a little low in confidence may find that they drive their confidence down even *further* by comparing themselves to the faster swimmers in their team, whereas some of the more *competitive* types often thrive on this, and improve even faster by comparing themselves to others. It all depends on what type of person you are, and your level of confidence in your own ability.

It's important to work out which category you fit into, as otherwise doing this may rip your confidence apart each time you are beginning to build it up again. In general, the majority of swimmers I have worked with have been better off focusing upon their own swim, and improving their *own* PB's - as this keeps them focused upon their own performance and off their competitors.

Mind Training for Swimmers

This fits in with my philosophy of 'focus upon the goal, not the obstacles' - but this is not to say that you might not be in the other category – but it's up to you to work this out for yourself.

One sure way of knowing the answer to this is if you find yourself *obsessing* about other swimmers' times, as this is a sure sign that you should bring your focus back in upon your *own* performance.

Never allow your competitors' performances to dominate your thinking however - your prime focus should always be your own lane, and your own swim. Otherwise, you may find your own performance is beginning to suffer due to lack of mental focus and attention - and this often occurs with *overly competitive* swimmers. These swimmers often want to win so much they almost try to *will their competitors to lose* rather than focus upon their performance - and this simply does not work.

If your goal becomes totally focused upon *another swimmer*, it renders your mind as useless during the race, as it is impossible for you to directly influence another swimmer's race with mental training.

Thoughts To Avoid Before Races

There are several different types of negative thoughts you must avoid before a race, any of which can de-rail your chances if you dwell upon these thoughts or allow them to strengthen and expand.

By avoiding and dealing with these negative thoughts, it becomes much easier to have a powerful focus, and a positive

Mind Training for Swimmers

expectancy about your races (because we get what we expect, not what we deserve).

There are several types of negative thoughts to watch out for, and some of these can be very subtle and slip into your mind right before a race without you even realizing. The first type to watch out for is uncontrollables - which we have discussed previously, which are thoughts about things which you have absolutely no control over whatsoever, and which are a total waste of energy.

The second form of negative thought is 'excuse-itis' and also 'negative expectancy'. These are negative thoughts, which seek out *reasons* why you may not perform well, and search for advance excuses *just in case* you happen to perform badly. Unfortunately, having an excuse in advance tends to become a self-fulfilling prophecy in the pool, bringing out very average performances - and are best avoided at all times.

Some examples of these thoughts include something like "if I don't swim a good time today, it's because I was sick last week", or "I probably won't be able to beat (Sarah/Joel), but I might be able to get 2nd or 3rd". Ensure you counteract this thinking by always focusing upon your goal, and expecting a positive outcome at all times.

Last of all, another subtle form of negative thought is what I call 'insurance thinking', where you might think to yourself something like "oh well, if I don't do well in this event, I still have the 200m this afternoon" - sort of like an insurance policy for failure. This is just a

Mind Training for Swimmers

subtle way of saying to yourself, "I give myself permission to fail", so obviously this is not a mindset that brings great results!

Always ensure you examine your thoughts before each race and check that no uncontrollables, excuse-itis, negative expectancy, or insurance thinking have crept into your mindset. If they do, eradicate those thoughts immediately and focus your mind back on what you *want,* instead of what you don't.

Your mind is incredibly powerful, but unfortunately unless it is directed and focused in the right direction, it can just as easily work against you - and with many swimmers, it often does. This is fine if it happens to your competitors of course, but just ensure it does not happen to you!

So make sure your mind is powering your body in the right direction - towards your goal, and this will always serve you best in the pool.

Develop An Expectation To Succeed

There is a particular saying that I tend to use a lot, because I like to ensure that swimmers will never forget it – and it's "swimmers don't get what they deserve - they get what they *expect"*. The reason that this is true is because *our deepest expectations tend to become reality* - due to our belief system being so enormously powerful.

This is one of the laws of the mind. So in order to get this law working *for* you - and not against you – it's highly important for you to actively work on creating a powerful mindset of *optimism,* which will

Mind Training for Swimmers

become your natural response to everything life happens to throw at you.

By practicing being optimistic – which is a very positive mindset - it becomes part of your everyday *belief system,* and it will automatically boost your results in the pool. Eventually you will begin to *expect the best* before every race – and this is generally what most positive, optimistic and determined swimmers, get.

Let's face it, those people who expect the worst are *almost always* right! This is because they have already programmed themselves for a bad result, and this is what they will continue to receive time and time again - until they manage to change their outlook.

Interestingly, people who think negatively also tend to attract *friends* who also think this way (and this group is not usually one of your highly successful groups of people!). Similarly, *positive upbeat* swimmers tend to attract other positive swimmers as friends - and this group is usually full of high achievers. Positive will always triumph over negative - maybe not always in the short term, but *always* in the long run.

Champion swimmers, at the deepest level, are always optimistic about their chances (yes, regardless of what they say to the media!). Because of their tremendous faith in their ability, they know that even when they are against the odds, they still have a chance - and a small chance is usually *all that a champion needs.*

We get what we expect, not what we deserve. History is strewn with thousands of examples of people who *put in all the work,* but never

Mind Training for Swimmers

received the grand payoff. If only they had known how to work with their minds, it might have been completely different for them. So make sure you use this information wisely – because some people would have given *anything* to have known this when they were competing.

So how do you create a mindset of optimism? It works simply by constantly working at it, every moment of the day. Life constantly provides you with thousands of opportunities where you have the choice to either think positively or negatively, and so you create a mindset that focuses upon the positive, and turns negatives into positives.

Being around happy, positive people also makes this much easier, as these types of people usually make you feel positive and optimistic just from being in their company – so be very choosey about the company you keep!

Your Mind And The Marshalling Area

Probably the No. 1 place where a swimmer becomes either *psyched up* or *psyched out* is in the marshalling area. I was giving a mental training seminar in Melbourne Australia once when I was asked by a young swimmer "What should I do when a competitor comes up to me in the marshalling area and asks me *what my best time is?*".

My answer was that whenever a swimmer asks you this question in the marshalling area, 99% of the time it means two things:

- That your competitor is *worried* about swimming against you; and

Mind Training for Swimmers

- They are going to try their very best to *psych you out* before the race starts!

Often questions by your competitors about your times – especially in the marshalling area - are usually designed to *mentally pull you down*. As soon as you tell them what your time is, they will most often inform you that they swam *faster* than your time last week - and this is purely designed to make you start worrying about *them* instead of focusing upon your own race.

So never, *ever* fall for this! Remember that they will say absolutely *whatever it takes* to make you feel more nervous before the race. In fact, they may not even be able to swim those times they say they can. But *even if they can,* it's not your job to focus upon your competitors, it's your job to focus upon your *own* swim – and let everyone else worry about *you.*

So never accept those negative thoughts into your mind before a race, because otherwise your conscious mind will *fuel* these thoughts and transform them into huge mental monsters before your race. You always have 100% choice over whether to accept these negative thoughts or not - always remember this - *you have the power to reject these comments at all times.*

In fact, when you think about it, it's actually a great *compliment* whenever a competitor tries to psych you out in the marshalling area (or anytime, really) as this means that they are *honestly and truly worried* about you as a competitor in their race.

Mind Training for Swimmers

Actually, this is exactly what you want – that is, your competitors focusing upon the *obstacles* – you - instead of their *goal*. But just ensure that you are ready for their mental tricks, and that you refuse to allow their feeble attempts to succeed in *shifting your focus away from your swim.* Think about your own race, and no one else's. Leave all the worrying to your competitors!

Now, if a competitor tries the more *direct* approach of intimidation, such as by saying something like, "I'm gonna kick your butt!" (a personal favourite of several swimmers, it seems!), once again this means that this swimmer is *really worried about you.* That's absolutely great! So never worry about these pathetic comments, or let them bother you - rise above them and just enjoy the fact that you know how scared they really are!

In these situations, the most important thing is actually what you *think,* not what you *say* to the other swimmer. For instance, if a swimmer asks you your times in the marshalling area, you might choose to tell them the truth, or you might choose to have a little fun and invent an even *better* time to give them - it doesn't matter and it's totally up to you, as it's *what you choose to think* which is most important.

Remember to always use *tunnel vision* in the marshalling room - this means to focus on your goal so much that you will never even *notice* the obstacles.

Mind Training for Swimmers

Keep Improving Your Mental Training

Never think that you know everything about your mind and body - it is important to keep improving your mental training. As time goes by, you may find that your mental training program needs to *evolve* with you. For instance, some techniques may not *feel* right for you anymore, or may need to be slightly changed in some way in order to keep them fresh, interesting and effective.

As *we* change, so do our mental training requirements - you may find you need a longer, shorter or more regular visualization, or that you need to change your affirmations, etc. The key is to keep thinking and noticing what *feels* right - because one thing is for sure, if it doesn't feel right, you probably won't be successful with it, or be able to maintain it.

So even though you have your Pre-Meet Mind Preparation, which is an excellent guide (and may well serve you all of your career), be *open* to changing some things if you find they don't work as well anymore.

Become your *own* mental trainer - because this is the ultimate swimmer, the person who knows his or her own mind and body better than anyone else. There comes a time when you must take responsibility for your own performance, and this includes maintaining your mental training with improvements along the journey.

Sleeping Problems Before Meets

Countless numbers of swimmers experience sleeping problems the night before a meet or big race. This occurs purely due to stress, and

Mind Training for Swimmers

the very fact that they find they can't fall asleep often creates *even more* stress for them, which makes sleeping even more difficult and their mind even more stressed.

The first thing to know is this - *don't worry* if you aren't falling asleep immediately. The odds are that you will still swim absolutely fine the next day. So number one is *don't stress yourself out* if you find yourself still awake some hours after going to bed.

So this means never, ever *write off your chances* in your race just because you slept badly. If you do this, your mind will use it as a ready-made excuse "just in case" you put in a poor swim, and this is not the mindset you want before a race.

Strangely enough, you might be interested to know that a bad night's sleep can actually make it quite possible to slip into *the zone,* and swim the greatest swim of your life! (And no, this is *not* to say that I am recommending late nights before meets or races!).

Yet so often when a swimmer has a bad night's sleep, or if they have been feeling ill during the week - their mind will *use this as an automatic excuse to swim badly,* and this is definitely *not* what you want. Having a ready-made excuse literally programs your mind with *permission to fail.* So never decide the outcome of your race in advance, until you have swum the race - you never know what miracles your mind and body are capable of bringing out.

OK, now we have that out of the way, let me give you some tips for a good night's sleep before meets! Here we go:

Mind Training for Swimmers

First of all, have a nice warm shower before going to bed, as this relaxes the mind and body before you get into bed and makes it easier to drift right off. However, if your mind seems very active when you get into bed, then read in bed for 20-30 minutes - preferably something *light, relaxing and easy* to read, definitely *not* study notes, schoolwork etc!

Then, find your favourite sleeping position, close your eyes and just *allow* yourself to drift off to sleep, never *force* it. Be OK with the fact that it might take a *few minutes, or even a few hours* before you drift off - and that either way, this is *just fine.* There must be no time limits or pressure put upon the time that you are to fall asleep, because the stress of time limits will only keep you awake.

If going to sleep does not seem *likely,* then imagine yourself being in your *sanctuary.* This is the "beautiful, safe place" that you normally imagine yourself in before your race visualization - but this time, just remain in this wonderful place – and leave swimming right out of it altogether. Your sanctuary is a place where you can feel calm, relaxed and where you have all the time in the world – perfect conditions for sleeping, but don't concentrate too hard on *seeing* the images, just *feel* that you are in this wonderful place.

This relaxing sanctuary can help produce the emotional feelings of *safety and security,* which also help to shut down the nervous adrenalin which the body produces each time you worry about tomorrow's race, which prevents you from drifting off to sleep.

Mind Training for Swimmers

Last but not least, if you are *still* awake, then try this - a silent mantra, which can work very well. Here's how you do it: While you lying in bed, each time you breathe in, you say to yourself the word "deeper...." (no, not aloud, just in your mind). Then, as you breathe out, say to yourself ".... and deeper" (or you can take out the "and" if you wish). So the mantra you are repeating to yourself "deeper.........and deeper,......deeper..........and deeper.....".

This is a very powerful but relaxing *mental command* for your mind to shut down and drift into the alpha, theta and delta states which produce sleep, which I use in many of my various hypnosis CDs.

However, be ready for a battle initially – because your conscious mind will try and fight this and do its best to continue thinking about tomorrow's meet, so be ready for this. Each and every time you discover your mind *thinking* again, gently but firmly return it back into reciting your mantra - again, again and again - until your mind *finally surrenders* and drifts off to sleep.

So relax, a bad night's sleep is *not* a death sentence for your PB the next day. Now you can go out there and show them who is boss.

The Ultimate Secret To All Swimming Success: Happiness

Do you enjoy training and swimming meets? Because here is an interesting fact that many do not realize - humans can ONLY truly succeed at things they enjoy.

This is because your very own subconscious mind's purpose is to move you *away* from pain, and towards pleasure. It's a natural human

Mind Training for Swimmers

instinct we simply cannot escape – and this is why, for instance, your reflexes instantaneously move your hand off a hot stove before it begins to burn, because your mind's job is to keep you out of harm.

This also means that to succeed in swimming (and life) we must do one of these two things; we must enjoy what we do, or otherwise, we have to find a *way* to enjoy it. So if you are not enjoying your swimming, it is essential to ask yourself why - and do whatever it takes to bring back the enjoyment.

Unhappiness has proven to bring failure, because it simply affects every major area of a swimmer's life - their emotional balance, motivation, perseverance, their relationships with coaches and other swimmers, and every other aspect of their training.

The major reasons for unhappiness I've encountered with swimmers include things such as boredom and lacking variety in their training, a personality clash with a coach or other swimmers, and being stressed out time-wise through other commitments such as work, school, family and social life.

If you ever begin to feel that you're losing your motivation, ask yourself why. If it has to do with your training, or a personality clash, talk to your coach and discuss it with them, to see if her or she can help. If it is your busy schedule, sit down and write out a new one, and see if you can fit in a little more relaxation. Life is too short not to enjoy what you are doing, and once again, if you really wish to succeed, your enjoyment is an essential ingredient - a plain and simple fact.

Mind Training for Swimmers

Put your own personal happiness at the very top of your priority list - and never, ever let it drop below number 1. Your motivation must always be there before you can make any serious attempt at achieving your goals. This does not mean that you will enjoy every waking second of swimming, but the main thing is to enjoy it overall. This applies to your life just as much as to your swimming!

If you love your swimming, then you're in the driver's seat - and you can't go wrong. But if you don't, find out why, and fix it. Never let anyone, or anything, affect your motivation - because this is the very thing that gets you out of bed every morning. Protect it, treasure it - because it's an essential part of who you really are.

Avoiding Burnout

Burnout is one of the very real threats to a successful swimmer's career, and it takes a very astute swimmer (and coach) to ensure they avoid this pitfall. Burnout has caused many great swimmers to end their careers prematurely, so it is vitally important you keep an eye out for signs of this to ensure it doesn't happen to you.

However, if you ever do experience burnout, as many champions have, you can also *move through it* and get back into the winner's circle. First of all, and needless to say, communication between the *swimmer and coach* is essential in this situation, as together you have to distinguish whether any signs of this are actually from *burnout*, and not just from plain *tiredness* - as these two can appear to be very much the same.

Mind Training for Swimmers

However, there are some distinct signs, which will separate tiredness from burnout - for instance, a swimmer who experiences *tiredness* will usually have *some* days where, even if they are still tired, they still manage to *enjoy* the training and will feel enthusiastic about the session.

However, a swimmer who is going through burnout will, often for weeks on end, get *no enjoyment whatsoever* from the training session, and find themselves constantly struggling physically and mentally with their sets and times - and this can go on for months. Of course, this has a major affect upon motivation and performance levels.

Energy loss or even a constant feeling of sadness about your swimming can also be symptoms to watch out for. In fact, the mind is so unbelievably powerful that, if a swimmer is experiencing burnout, it may even create cold or flu-like symptoms in their body - purely to *keep them out of the pool* for a while. Your subconscious will always do whatever it takes to look after you, and so if it thinks you need a rest from the pool, it will make sure you get one!

So always remember that your *enjoyment, appreciation and enthusiasm* for swimming are hugely important aspects to your motivation and future success in the pool, and you should cultivate these as much as possible. If you find these have been *completely missing* from your training for some time, it's important to chat to your coach about it - as success can only truly come from something you enjoy.

Amongst other possibilities, your coach may choose to put *increased variety* into your training sets in order to help combat this

Mind Training for Swimmers

situation, or possibly even ask you to take a little *time off* to rekindle your enthusiasm and energy.

Burnout can come from several sources. It may even be that a particular goal you are striving for, such as to win a particular event at a meet, might be causing you to become *too emotionally attached* to the goal, which causes great stress and slow times. If this happens, it's best to take your focus *off* the goal for a while and direct it onto something else. (And believe it or not, this will most probably give you a *better chance* of performing well at the meet, as well).

The other thing to keep in mind is never to *dwell* on disappointing results for too long - *learn* from them, but then always *shift* your focus onto your *next* goal, and leave the past behind, where it belongs. (Of course, if you swim brilliantly, dwell upon the result as long as you like!). The past can only affect you if you choose to focus upon it.

So monitor your enjoyment and energy levels regularly to ensure you don't experience burnout. But if this ever happens, remember that you can always move through it - by increasing the variety in your swimming (and chatting to you coach), taking some focus *off* any goals which may be stressing you, focusing on *new* goals instead of past disappointments, and possibly even taking some time off. So my best advice for now is: Go out there and enjoy every stroke!

Mind Training for Swimmers

Moving To A New Team

If you are not moving to a new team and do not need to read this section, go forward to the next chapter, Chapter 17 – "Your Mental Training Program".

Moving to a new team can be a fabulous thing but it can also bring some new *additional* pressures which swimmers are not always prepared for. So I will highlight a few of these pressures to help you prepare for them, so you can cope, relax and swim better whenever you are in this transition situation.

Obviously there will be the whole new *workout and coaching* side of things which you will need to get accustomed to, both in and out of the pool, which takes some time - but also there is the highly-underestimated *personal* side of changing teams which can have a major affect on your morale if you are not watchful. These areas include formulating new friendships and training buddies, dealing with jealousy and often the unfortunate *loss* of close friends from the old team that you have left behind.

Needless to say, the *workout and coaching* scenario can be completely different to what you are used to, and may sometimes emphasize areas of your swimming, event selection, strokes and dry land training that you have not focused on much before, so be prepared for some changes as this can take some time to fully acclimatize in these areas.

On the mental side of things, some swimmers find that *leaving old friends behind* from your old club can initially affect morale, and

Mind Training for Swimmers

make the transition of changing clubs unexpectedly more difficult - but know that (most often) these feelings are only temporary, and 99 per cent of the time, you *will* acclimatize to your new club over the months ahead and make new friends.

Why is this important, you may ask? Because swimmers *almost always* swim best when they are in a happy frame of mind - so keeping up your morale is a hugely important factor for your swimming performances.

Of course, with all the various forms of communication these days such as email, chat, mobile phones etc - nobody needs to *completely* lose touch with old friends anymore, though be prepared to realize that in some of these old friendships, the boundaries may change due to you changing clubs.

Regrettably, in some cases old team-mates may view your move to another club as an act of betrayal, and no longer be prepared to remain as close as before - but try not to dwell on this for too long, as there will always be new friends that will come along, plus most of the time, this process simply weeds out those people who are your real friends anyway!

Another aspect that you may encounter at a new club is occasional jealousy from some of your (new) team mates - especially if some feel that you are *taking away some of the attention* they normally receive from the coach or other team mates.

Sometimes this simply cannot be avoided, but it can also help *not* to assume that every member of the team is going to be overjoyed to

Mind Training for Swimmers

see you in the first week - so take it slowly when building up your new friendships, and remain close initially with any swimmers you may already know on the new team.

Sometimes having a great reputation as a swimmer can make this jealousy situation *even more* difficult initially when you change clubs, however the good news is that it can also open a few doors as well!

However the main thing to know is that if you find the change difficult initially, know that it *will get easier* - just give it some time. Invariably you will begin to feel like part of the team, create new friends and begin to truly relax - and sure enough, you will bring out your best times for all to see.

CHAPTER 17

Your Mental Training Program

This is your mental training program to begin working on *from today onwards*. It takes no more than around 15 minutes out of your day, but will be the best investment in your swimming you could possibly make.

I have specified a minimum time period for each of these techniques, after which you can choose to *continue, add to, or change* to your own requirements. I have also recommended ways you can tailor these techniques for later use.

Here is your Mental Training Program:

- Daily Visualization for 10-15 minutes, for a minimum of 6 weeks.

  This is essential. Schedule the time to do your visualization each day. Tick off the days you have done the exercise on a calendar. Monitor your results, and after the 42 days you *may* reduce it to 8-12 minutes a day if you wish. An additional 5-10 minute visualization before races would also be highly recommended

Mind Training for Swimmers

when you can. Visualization is one of the most crucial parts of the program. If you are using the CD visualization, consider *alternating* it every second day *after the first 30 days,* with the use of a self-made music CD / iPod. This is not essential if you feel that you are not becoming over-familiar with the exercise.

- Affirmations - daily, plus before races

Mentally repeat a daily affirmation (the one you chose earlier in the affirmations chapter), a minimum of 3 minutes a day, *for the first eight (8) weeks.*

This is to help condition your mind for success, and also helps to achieve long-term goals quicker and overcome long-term problems. These can be done at intervals anytime throughout the day, whenever you have a moment to yourself. After this eight-week period, you can either *maintain* this schedule (which is recommended), or reduce it down to *every second day,* or (at the absolute minimum) *3 minutes daily during the 2 weeks before meets.*

You can change your affirmation at any time and swap to another, or you can use 2 affirmations on the same day if you wish.

- Mentally repeat an affirmation of your choice a minimum of 3 minutes a day, for *two weeks before every meet.*

When tailoring this method later, it's recommended not to reduce

Mind Training for Swimmers

this to any less than a week before the meet.

- Mentally repeat a pre-race affirmation directly before *every* race for 5-10 minutes.
  Recite an affirmation of your choice, preferably focused upon *speed or confidence.* Please note this is an *ongoing* part of the training.

- Create a Positive New Thought Pattern, with a 4 week Mental Diet.
  Notice, cancel, and replace all negative *thoughts and statements* as soon as they arise. Watch the words and statements you choose for the next 4 weeks - are they positive? Replace negative words and statements with more positive ones. Refuse to get *emotionally involved* in any negative thoughts, just let them wither and die from lack of attention. Refuse to think or accept negative thoughts, just keep continually throwing them out. After this four-week period, continue to monitor your thoughts - much of this monitoring will have become *automatic* by this time, however you will still have to consciously cancel the thoughts. This also includes not getting emotionally involved in, or fuelling, negative thoughts.

Recommended Option: Extending the Mental Diet to 2 months.

Mind Training for Swimmers

- Success List Before Every Meet

  Buy a ruled exercise book, and create your Success List. Use this *at least once during the week before each meet*, taking the time to truly allow the memory of each event to come back to your conscious mind.

- Practice Periodically Reaching 'The Zone' In Training For The Next 8 Weeks.

  Work at trying to reach 'the zone' in *particular sets* of our training (but not every set). Also, if you have an important meet coming up shortly, practice this sparingly and postpone the main practice of it until after the meet is over. However, the sooner you can master this, the sooner you can begin to use it in your meets.

- Body Language

  Begin working on your body language and attitude at meets, and at gradually transforming into "The Machine" - the swimmer who sees everything as a 'positive' and is totally unaffected by negatives and setbacks. Once you reach this point, very little will be able to get in your way.

- Mood Chart (optional extra)

  This is something you may choose to do now, or at a later date. It is highly worth finding out what your Peak Emotional State is.

Mind Training for Swimmers

Important: This entire mental training program works successfully for virtually all swimmers, especially those who stick diligently to the program. It has also shown to my knowledge *not* to have any negative affects of any kind over the years I have been teaching it. Of course, everyone is different - so if for any reason you feel that a particular method in the program seems to create a noticeable *negative* reaction of any kind, please *discontinue* that particular method, and monitor your progress to decide whether it was that method which made the difference. If so, discontinue the method altogether.

Your Pre-Meet Mental Preparation

Here is a checklist of mental preparation for the 1-2 weeks before every meet.

- Minimum once daily 10-15 minute visualization of your *main events in your next meet* during the 2 weeks before. (Occasional visualizations of other races are also OK). Additional 5-30 second 'flashes' of visualization can be used periodically during the day if you find you have some time.
- Daily affirmations in the 2 weeks before the meet, a minimum of 3 minutes of repetitions each day. Also, recite affirmations for 3-10 minutes before every race.

Mind Training for Swimmers

- In the week before a meet, ensure that you do not get emotionally upset about anything. Avoid arguments, problems, confrontations etc, and take care of them *after the meet is over.*

- Be very aware of keeping your thoughts as positive as possible, especially during the 2 weeks before the meet. Avoid being negative in any way, seeing your whole life as being fun, easy and harmonious.

- Remind yourself that the meet will be a *fun challenge,* not a scary ordeal.

- Begin acting like a champion in your body language and attitude.

- Use your Success List at least once during the week before the meet, to re-create that winning feeling.

- Read the Pre-Race Psych-Up before your race (Chapter 16).

- Remind yourself often that the other swimmers have YOU to worry about!

- Schedule some fun and relaxation in the week before the meet - relaxing things where you can completely forget about swimming for a while. eg. A movie. You do not want to be thinking about the race every waking moment, as this can sap your mental energy.

Mind Training for Swimmers

Things Worth Remembering

- You are always in control of your own performance - your mind controls your body, and you control your mind! Never forget this.

- Nervousness is normal, so don't worry about it - expect it, handle it, and channel it into your swim. No one can ever affect you unless you choose to let him or her. Your attitude is 100% your own responsibility (and no-one else's fault). Guard your thoughts carefully.

- The most vital part of swimming is *your own belief in yourself.* Boost yourself up before races! Occasional slumps are normal, so don't worry too much about these. Just use your mental training techniques to help move yourself out of it. Any obstacles in your way are only important if you choose to focus upon them.

- Never *imagine* things going wrong - this is a powerful form of 'negative visualization', and it works really effectively! Always change the mental pictures to positive ones.

- You are responsible for your own thoughts - powerful thoughts bring powerful performances, junk thoughts deliver junk performances.

Mind Training for Swimmers

- Admire other successful people - jealous people are rarely successful! Stay out of all jealous gossip about other team members.

Daily Maintenance

It's now time to begin (if you haven't already) your four-week mental diet of weeding the negatives from the garden of your mind. This includes watching for negative words in your everyday vocabulary, and replacing them with positives. To be a winner, you must think and talk like one - this means choosing positive words and sentences, and getting rid of negative thoughts from your mind.

This is vital for anyone to achieve anything important, and to a certain extent, will become an aspect that you will have to monitor for the rest of your swimming career. An untended garden soon gets way out of control. Once you have cleared out most of the self-sabotage (which almost everyone possesses), you will be very difficult to stop!

Mental Training Checklist - For The Future

This checklist is so you can highlight the areas you may still have to work on in the future - in the weeks, months and years ahead, especially during times when things are not going as well as you would like.

This should help to jog your memory about the important topics you may need to re-read as well. Make a point of noting the techniques

Mind Training for Swimmers

on which you still need to work.

Mental Training Checklist:

- Are you using visualization regularly?
- Do you have any bad performances from the past that still bother you? If so, have you worked on erasing them using the visualization technique?
- Have you tried customizing the imagery in your visualizations?
- Are you getting into a relaxed state when you visualize?
- Do you recite affirmations for 5-10 minutes before races?
- Have you created (and do you use) your Success List?
- Have you updated it, since you created it?.
- Do you know your own Peak Emotional State?
- Are you worrying about 'uncontrollables' at meets?
- Do you watch your thoughts and speech for 'negatives'?
- Do you cancel out negative thoughts as they arise?
- Do you feel intimidated by other swimmers?
- If so, have you tried overcoming this with visualization techniques?
- Do you have goals to aim for? Have you written them down?
- Are you moving closer to, or further away from, your goals?

Mind Training for Swimmers

- If so, are you trying too hard, and too emotionally attached to your goal?
- Have you been 'in the zone' yet?
- If not, are you practicing this in training?
- Do you think of meets as a *fun challenge*, or as an ordeal?
- Do you avoid getting emotionally upset before races, such as arguments?
- Do you avoid negative people before races, to keep yourself positive?
- Are you able to focus on your lane only, forgetting about anyone else's?
- Do you get overly disappointed when you don't achieve your goal?
- Do you mentally boost yourself up before races?
- Is your body language positive, like that of a champion?
- Do you think the way a champion would think?
- Do you look at the pool conditions at meets and say 'this is great'?
- Have you tried 'delaying the pain' in training?
- Are you focusing on your goal, or the obstacles in your way?
- Do you ask "what's great about this?" at meets?
- Do you have a good relationship and communication with your coach?

- Do you ask them about your progress, or if you need to make any changes?

Go through this list regularly, to see where you could be improving further in future. Here is your summary for this chapter.

Summary

- Begin using your Mental Training Program from today, make a start immediately and begin to condition your subconscious for success.
- Use the Mental Training Checklist in the future to discover the areas of your mental training you may need to give more attention.

The Three Phases of Training

Well, this wraps up the Study phase of your program, now comes the Practice phase, where you must now put the techniques of the program into action. Making this first step of the Practice phase is the *most* important or you may never reach the final phase - so begin now! Do not 'leave it a couple of days' or you may never begin it at all.

If you are disciplined enough to stay on this program as directed, the Practice phase may bring some great results for you, even possibly during the first month - but remember to be patient! It's long-term success we want, *not* short-term miracles.

Mind Training for Swimmers

The third and final phase is the Mastery phase, and this is where you reap most of the benefits from your mental training program. During this phase you often become highly aware of your mental and physical state (as well as your competitors'), and become able to troubleshoot problems before they eventuate. During this phase results begin to flow nicely for you and your confidence and self-belief become very strong and unwavering.

But to reach this phase, you have to get to work now, on the Practice phase! So don't delay, begin endeavouring to make yourself as mentally powerful as you are physically, and watch as your results improve dramatically.

I hope that I'll be reading about your performances in the future, and watching you give interviews on television! Begin now, and show the world what you can do.

P.S. Best of luck (not that you should need it, once you put these principles into action!), and remember to aim to do the 10-15 minute visualization technique daily for 42 days. After this your mind should be well conditioned for success and in a good routine, and so if you wish, you can reduce it to 8-12 minutes each day. This exercise alone can bring results if you have the discipline and patience required to do it. For information regarding the CD see:

www.swimpsychology.com/swim_CD.php3

I hope you have enjoyed this book, and are ready to begin your mental training program - that is, if you have not already started!   I'd love to hear any of your comments you may have about the book, the

Mind Training for Swimmers

program, or especially any fabulous results you have achieved using it – you can contact me by email through my swim website or through www.MindTraining.net. Good luck with your journey, I'll see you at the top!

Quotation References

Page 13 - Leisl Jones quote from Sun Herald newspaper article courtesy of Janelle Miles (AAP Brisbane) July 11, 2004.

Page 155 - Extract from "Swimming Against the Tide" by Petria Thomas reprinted by permission of the Australian Broadcasting Corporation and ABC Books. (c) 2005 ABC. All rights reserved.

CPSIA information can be obtained
at www.ICGtesting.com
Printed in the USA
BVHW071120280220
573632BV00002B/173

9 780977 191680